JAPANESE FOR BUSY PEOPLE I
THE WORKBOOK

JAPANESE FOR BUSY PEOPLE

I

THE WORKBOOK
DRILLS FOR ORAL FLUENCY

Association for Japanese-Language Teaching

KODANSHA INTERNATIONAL
Tokyo • New York • London

Distributed in the United States by Kodansha America, Inc., 114 Fifth
Avenue, New York, N.Y. 10011, and in the United Kingdom and conti-
nental Europe by Kodansha Europe, Ltd., Gillingham House, 38–44
Gillingham Street, London SW1V 1HU.

Published by Kodansha International Ltd., 17–14 Otowa 1-chome,
Bunkyo-ku, Tokyo 112, and Kodansha America, Inc. Copyright © 1993
by the Association for Japanese-Language Teaching. All rights
reserved. Printed in Japan.
ISBN 4–7700–1709–X

First edition, 1993

93 94 95 10 9 8 7 6 5 4 3 2 1

CONTENTS

INTRODUCTION

Japanese for Busy People I was prepared for people who do not have a lot of time to study and thus need an efficient way of learning basic grammar and expressions appropriate to various situations. We felt, however, that additional material in the form of oral drills would be helpful in enabling students to speak Japanese at normal conversational speed. This is a skill that mere amassment of knowledge *about* a language cannot confer.

As a result, we have developed this collection of drills to provide practice in the material in *Japanese for Busy People I*. This workbook can be used in class as a supplement for introducing or reviewing lessons, and outside the classroom for homework and review. In fact, it is recommended that drills be used both in the classroom, and then outside it for the purpose of reinforcement. When coordinated with the exercises and quizzes in the main textbook, the workbook should enable students to improve their command of basic Japanese in a relatively short time.

This book has been prepared by Akiko Kajikawa and Junko Shinada, teachers at the Association for Japanese-Language Teaching (AJALT), with the advice of Shigeko Miyazaki, Miyako Iwami, and Haruko Matsui, and the assistance of Yōko Hattori, Hiroko Kuroda, and Harumi Mizuno, all of whom are AJALT teachers.

How to Use the Workbook

The workbook has not been prepared to ascertain whether students have mastered the lessons in the main text but to provide practice in various aspects of them: understanding sentence structure (sentence pattern drills), understanding the usage of sentences and expressions (situation drills), and learning vocabulary (vocabulary drills).

Using cues in the form of pictures and charts—but without sample sentences—the drills will elicit Japanese words, sentences, and expressions from the student. In sentence pattern drills, this method of presentation should motivate students to construct and use realistic sentences on their own, rather than encourage the mindless substitution of words in a sample sentence. Practicing sentences in this way should thus foster a better understanding of the sentence structure of Japanese. In situation drills, working without a sample sentence should enhance students' ability to come up with sentences appropriate to the situation based on the Japanese they already know, and make it less likely that they will merely be memorizing sentences.

The drills should be done orally and repeated until the words and sentences come smoothly. The blank right-hand pages are for any notes you may wish to make.

Sentence Pattern Drills

L6-1, 2, 3, 4
Drill L6 is the first drill in the book for mastering the basic structure of sentences with verbs. Since such sentences can be complex, we begin with simple elements and build on them, as follows:

1. Destination
2. Subject + destination + verb
3. Subject + destination + verb ā time
4. Subject + destination + verb ā time ā person accompanying the subject

The four segments of Drill L6 use the above sequence. Drill L6-1 has the student memorize destinations, with the instructor first giving the words *"ginkō," "Fuji-san,"* and *"Furansu"* as examples. Students should repeat the words and phrases until they are mastered.

Drill L6-2 provides practice with the pattern . . . *wa* . . . *ni ikimasu/kaerimasu,* together with other tenses and interrogative patterns. The instructor should first briefly introduce Bijī-san, the subject of the drill, and give as a model sentence *"Ashita Bijī-san wa ginkō ni ikimasu,"* based on Picture 1. Students should then begin making sentences, starting with Picture 2 and going all the way to Picture 9. Take note that students should switch to the past tense at Picture 5, to an interrogative sentence at Picture 8, and to the appropriate form of the verb *kaeru* at Picture 9. If a student makes a mistake, point this out and lead the student to the correct form, or give a grammatical explanation if necessary, before having the student repeat the sentence. Drill for fluency.

Drills L6-3, 4 provide practice with the pattern . . . *to* . . . *ni ikimasu/kaerimasu.* The pattern of presentation is the same as that for the preceding drill. Once students can make up their own sentences using the pictures in this drill, it is safe to assume that they understand the basic structure of sentences that contain verbs.

L7-2
This drill has students explain the schedule depicted using sentence patterns they have already learned. Instructors may wish to make a schedule in Japanese for students who have trouble memorizing vocabulary. The instructor should begin by asking such questions as *"Tanaka-san wa getsu-yōbi ni doko ni ikimasu ka"* to ascertain that students are following the presentation, and should then have the students explain the schedule in Japanese. Encourage the students to make such long sentences as *"Getsu-yōbi no jūni-ji ni takushī de Sumisu-san to Tōkyō Hoteru ni ikimasu."*

Listen for correct grammar and pronunciation and natural speed as the students say the sentences elicited by the drills. Natural rhythm can be reinforced by making reference to the Answer Section at the back of the book (using the slashes that divide the sentences into segments and clapping or tapping lightly on the desk to emphasize the rhythm). If there is not enough time in class to complete the drills, they may be assigned for oral homework. The drills may also be effectively used as review exercises.

Situation Drills

Situation drills provide practice in how certain expressions function in various situations. Once students have grasped the connection between the situation and the expression in a given drill, they should practice the drill until they are fluent in the expressions. Instructors should enhance the reality of the situations by using appropriate props and encourage students to pronounce the phrases with the emotion appropriate to the situation.

L13-2

The instructor should first have the students read the English background and instructions at the top of the page and then have them come up with expressions appropriate to the situations depicted. Drill for fluency. If possible, such props as a picture or an old clock should be brought to the classroom to lend reality to the situations. This drill should be useful for homework, review, and testing as well.

L16-1

This drill has students supply the appropriate expressions for the balloons of the cartoons. Such drills provide a means for practicing the flow of a conversation; once the basic pattern is learned, conversations in real situations will be easier.

First, have students read the background sentence at the top of the page, then ask them to think up appropriate expressions for each of the frames. Once correct expressions are selected, drill for fluency.

Vocabulary Drills

L13-1, 2

The purpose of these drills is to learn adjectives. Although the drill may be used in various ways, the most effective places a minimal burden on the students and builds from there, as follows:

1. The instructor says *"Ōkii,"* and points to the appropriate picture.
2. The instructor says *"Ōkii,"* and the student points to the appropriate picture.
3. The student says the adjective, and the instructor points to the appropriate picture.
4. The instructor points to the picture, and the student says the adjective.

The drill can be expanded by dividing the words into groups of *-i* and *-na* adjectives, by having students recite the negative forms of the adjectives, and by having them say the adjectives with nouns.

Notes

1. The numbers of the lessons in this workbook correspond to the numbers of lessons in *Japanese for Busy People I*. The vocabulary in the drills generally corresponds to that in the lessons, but additional words are included, which are shown in boxes.

2. As noted previously, no sample sentences are provided in the drills. People studying on their own should refer to the appropriate lesson in *Japanese for Busy People I* if they are not sure of the basic sentence pattern or expression to use.

3. Answers to the drills are found at the back of the book.

Use of the Answer Section for Pronunciation Practice

The sentences in the Answer Section are divided into segments using slash marks (/). Designed to provide a guide to natural pronunciation, this way of dividing sentences is known as the Verbo-Tonal Method, or VTM. It was devised in the 1950s by Dr. Pedal Gubrina, a professor at Sarajevo University in Yugoslavia.

To make the most effective use of the method, first pronounce the word(s) between two slashes as a unit, without taking a breath or halting. Say each unit with the same average time. You may find it helpful to tap out the rhythm with your fingers. With practice, this method should enable you to speak Japanese with a natural rhythm.

L1-1

1. *"Nihon."* Say this word as a unit.

2. *"Chū/goku."* Say *Chū - goku* with two-part time, as two separate units. If this word is pronounced as a single unit from the outset, the long vowel of the first element is likely to be too short. Once the two units are pronounced correctly, practice saying the word as a single unit.

3. *"Doi/tsu."* First say *doi* and *tsu* as two separate units to ensure that the *tsu*, which is liable to be pronounced too short, is given its natural length. Once the two units are pronounced correctly, practice saying the word as a single unit.

L1-2

1. *"Kochira wa/Tōkyō/Denki no/Tanaka-san/desu."* Once the sentence can be pronounced with a natural rhythm using these divisions, the units can be expanded to *"Kochira wa/Tōkyō Denki no/Tanaka-san desu."*

THE WORKBOOK

Lesson 1–1

Countries and Nationalities

Look at the following map and give the names of all the countries, followed by the respective nationalities.

United Kingdom, **Igirisu**, JBP I, p. 49
France, **Furansu**, JBP I, p. 49

14

Lesson 1–2

Introducing Someone

Introduce each of the following acquaintances to your Japanese colleague, Mr. Hayashi.

1
Tokyo Electric Co., Ltd.
Haruo Tanaka

2
Berlin Bank
Hans Hoffman

3
French Embassy
Bruno Dupont

4
*London Securities
Kate Brown

5
Berlin Bank
Secretary
Keiko Suzuki

6
ABC
Lawyer
David Smith

7
*Tokyo University
Student
Lin Shu-rei

London Securities, **Rondon Shōken**
Tokyo University, **Tōkyō Daigaku**

Lesson 2

Telephone Numbers

Give the office telephone number, and then the home telephone number, shown on each person's namecard.

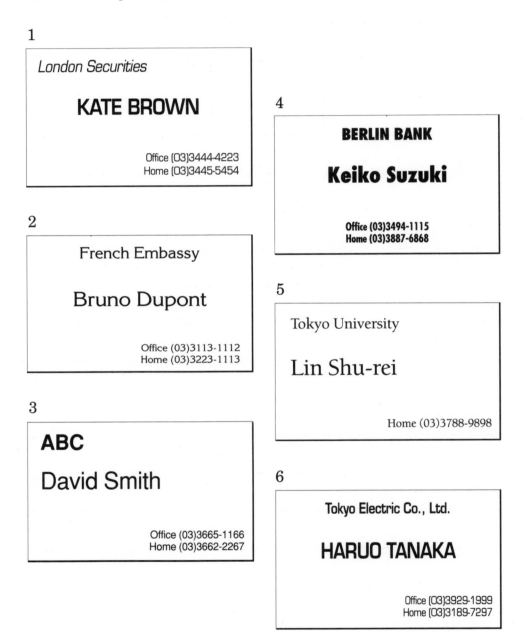

1

London Securities

KATE BROWN

Office (03)3444-4223
Home (03)3445-5454

2

French Embassy

Bruno Dupont

Office (03)3113-1112
Home (03)3223-1113

3

ABC

David Smith

Office (03)3665-1166
Home (03)3662-2267

4

BERLIN BANK

Keiko Suzuki

Office (03)3494-1115
Home (03)3887-6868

5

Tokyo University

Lin Shu-rei

Home (03)3788-9898

6

Tokyo Electric Co., Ltd.

HARUO TANAKA

Office (03)3929-1999
Home (03)3189-7297

Lesson 3–1

Telling the Time

Give the times shown in pictures 1 through 12, and then the opening hours or showing times in pictures 13 through 16.

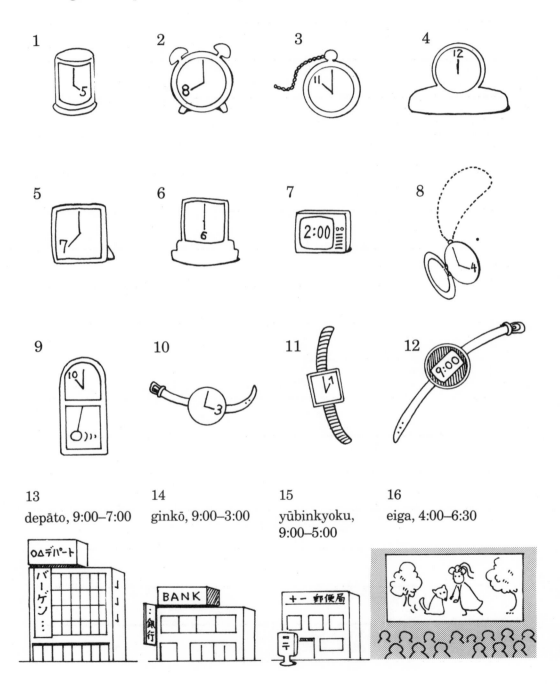

13
depāto, 9:00–7:00

14
ginkō, 9:00–3:00

15
yūbinkyoku,
9:00–5:00

16
eiga, 4:00–6:30

Lesson 3–2

Schedule (1)

Describe the following schedule.

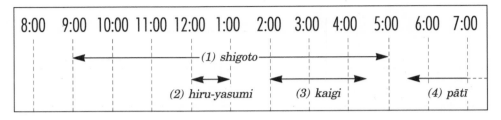

Lesson 3–3

Schedule (2)

Describe the following schedule.

SUN	MON	TUE	WED	THU	FRI	SAT
	1 *(1) tanjōbi* *Mr. Suzuki*	**2**	**3**	**4**	**5**	**6**
7	**8**	**9**	**10**	**11**	**12**	**13**
14	**15**	**16**	**17**	**18**	**19**	**20** *(4) tanjōbi* *Mr. Hayashi*
21	**22**	**23**	**24** *(5) *gorufu*	**25**	**26**	**27**
28	**29**	**30**	**31**			

(2) natsu-yasumi (between 1 and 6)

*(3) *shutchō* (between 15 and 20)

| **shutchō**, business trip |
| **gorufu**, golf, JBP I, p. 106 |

Lesson 4

How Much?

Give the prices of the following items.

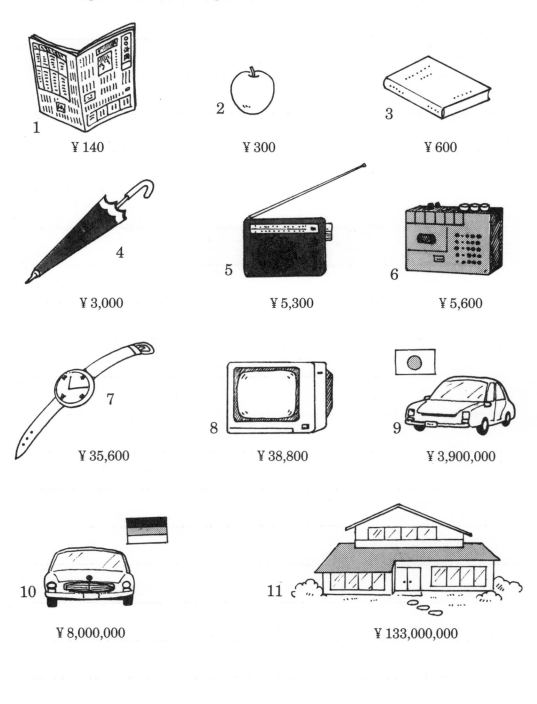

1 ¥ 140

2 ¥ 300

3 ¥ 600

4 ¥ 3,000

5 ¥ 5,300

6 ¥ 5,600

7 ¥ 35,600

8 ¥ 38,800

9 ¥ 3,900,000

10 ¥ 8,000,000

11 ¥ 133,000,000

Lesson 5

Shopping

Ask for the following items.

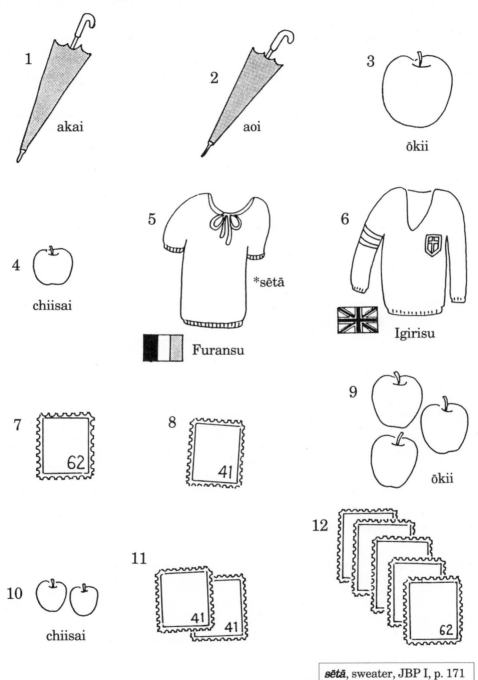

1 akai

2 aoi

3 ōkii

4 chiisai

5 *sētā — Furansu

6 Igirisu

7 62

8 41

9 ōkii

10 chiisai

11 41 41

12 62

sētā, sweater, JBP I, p. 171

Lesson 6–1

Place Names

Memorize the following words or names.

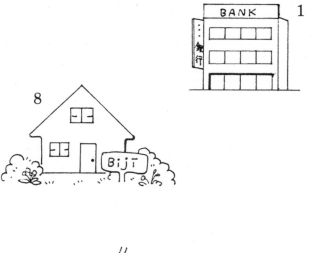

1

2

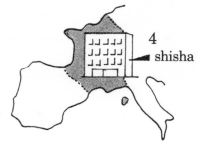

3

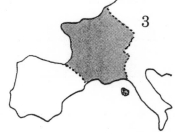

4

shisha

8

7

6

tomodachi

5

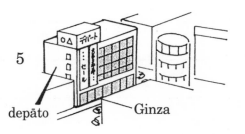

depāto

Ginza

Lesson 6–2

Going Somewhere

Describe Mr. Bijī's actions in the pictures.

Mr. Bijī
—is a very busy business man.
—is an American.
—resides in Japan.
—is thirty years old.

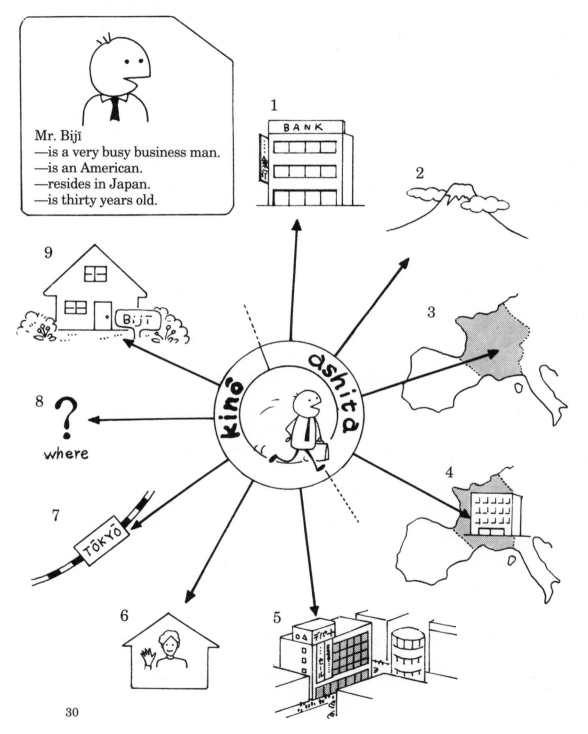

Lesson 6–3

Going Somewhere with Someone (1)

Describe Mr. Bijī's actions in the pictures.

Lesson 6–4

Going Somewhere with Someone (2)

Student A should ask Student B as many questions as possible regarding pictures 1 through 6, and Student B should answer.

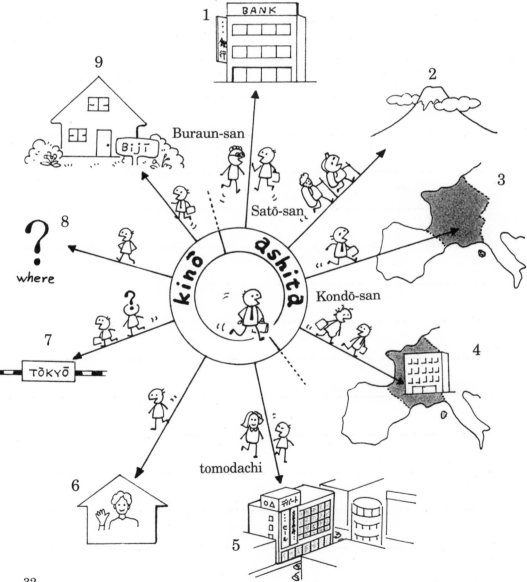

Lesson 6–5

At a Bus Stop

Make up a suitable dialogue.

Lesson 7–1

Means of Transport

Describe the actions shown in the pictures, including the time and means of transport.

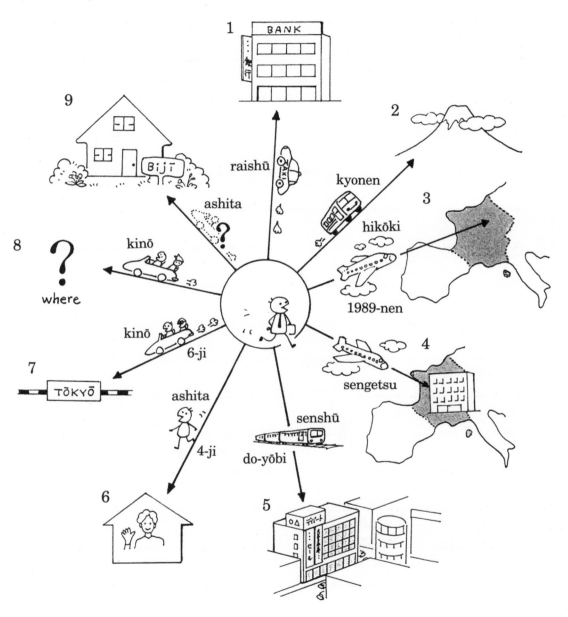

Lesson 7–2

Mr. Tanaka's Schedule (1)

Describe Mr. Tanaka's schedule for the coming week.

1	Mon.	12:00 4:00	Tokyo Hotel (by taxi, with Mr. Smith) London Securities, Tokyo branch (by taxi)
2	Tue.	 7:00	OFF Hakone (by car, with the *family) Return home
3	Wed.		Go to Osaka branch (by airplane, alone)
4	Thu.		Go to Kyoto branch (with someone from the Osaka branch) Return to Tokyo (by Shinkansen)
5	Fri.	12:00 4:00 6:00	Restaurant (with secretary) Go to ABC (with Mr. Hayashi) American Embassy
6	Sat.	1:00 7:00	Department store (with Mrs. Tanaka) Friend's house (with Mrs. Tanaka)
7	Sun.	9:00 2:00	*Park (with friends) Friends coming to my home

family, **kazoku**, JBP I, p. 83
park, **kōen**, JBP I, p. 95

Lesson 8–1

Who and What Is Where (1)

Describe who or what is where in the building below, starting from the first floor.

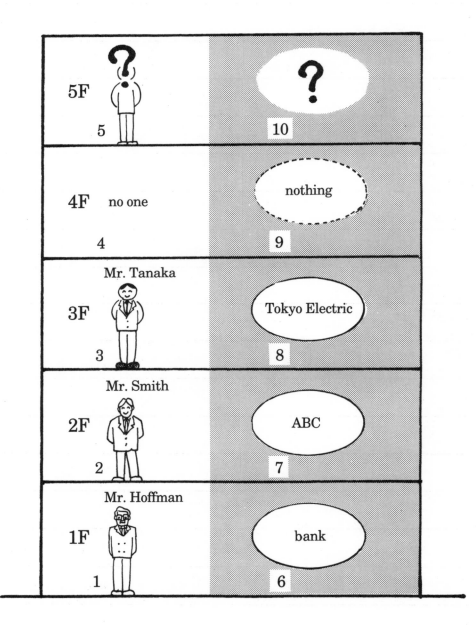

Lesson 8–2

A House Floor Plan

Describe the position of the rooms in the floor plan, starting to the left of the dining room, then describe the items in the rooms.

migi, right, JBP I, p. 138
hidari, left, JBP I, p. 139
e, picture, JBP I, p. 83
sofā, sofa
reizōko, refrigerator,
furoba, bathroom
kansōki, dryer
sentakuki, washing machine

Lesson 9–1

Who and What Is Where (2)
Name the items indicated, saying where and how many of them there are.

kaban, bag

Lesson 9–2

Where Is It?

Describe where items 1 through 8 are, and then where the organizations/facilities 9 through 16 are.

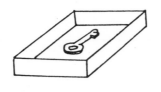

1 kagi

2 megane

3 denwa

4 kasa

5 shimbun

6 haizara

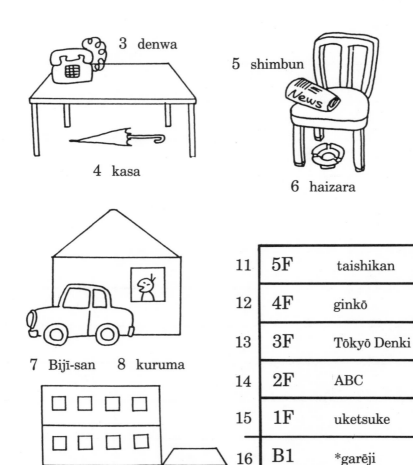

7 Bijī-san   8 kuruma

9 resutoran   10 hon-ya

11	5F	taishikan
12	4F	ginkō
13	3F	Tōkyō Denki
14	2F	ABC
15	1F	uketsuke
16	B1	*garēji

garēji, garage

Lesson 10–1

Daily Activities (1)

Memorize the verbs for the following actions.

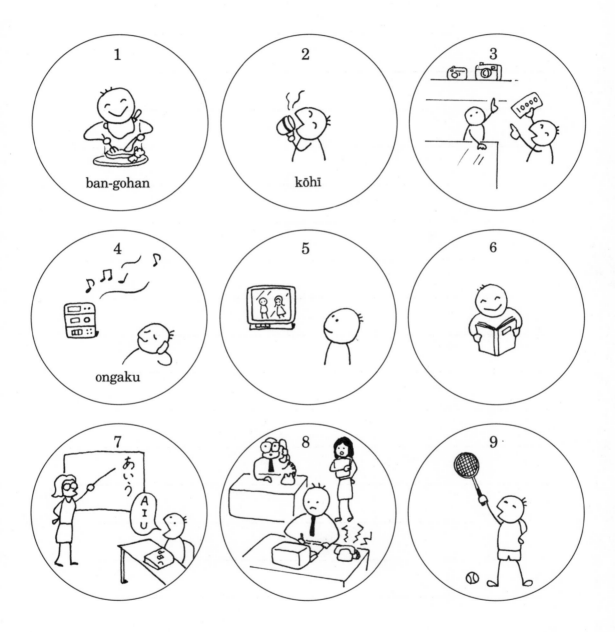

1 ban-gohan

2 kōhī

3

4 ongaku

5

6

7

8

9

Lesson 10–2

Daily Activities (2)

Describe what Mr. Bijī does and where he does it.

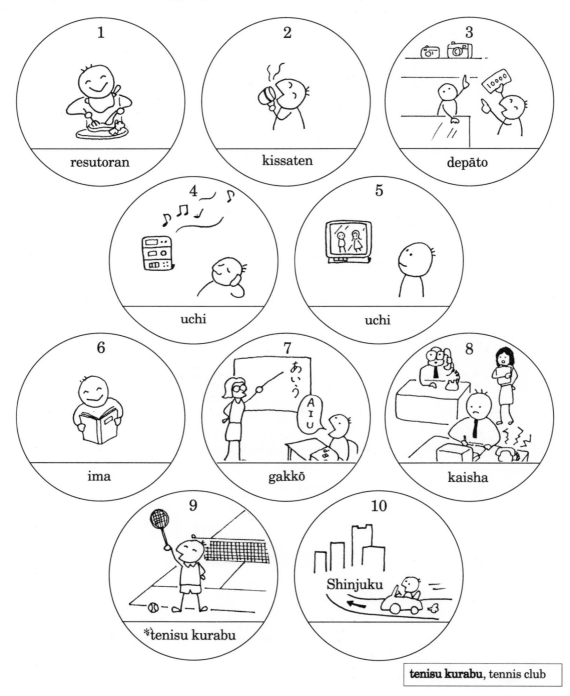

1 resutoran

2 kissaten

3 depāto

4 uchi

5 uchi

6 ima

7 gakkō

8 kaisha

9 *tenisu kurabu

10 Shinjuku

tenisu kurabu, tennis club

Lesson 10–3

Daily Activities (3)

1. Describe what Mr. Bijī is going to do and where he is going to do it.

2. Student A should ask Student B as many questions as possible regarding pictures 1 through 10, and Student B should answer.

sutēki, steak
bā, bar
wain, wine
uisukī, whisky

Lesson 10–4

Mr. Tanaka's Schedule (2)

Describe Mr. Tanaka's schedule for the coming week.

1	Mon.	8:00 | 9:00 12:00 4:00 | 5:00	*Meeting (office) Lunch (Tokyo Hotel, with Mr. Smith) Meeting (London Securities, Tokyo branch)
2	Tue.	 7:00 8:00	OFF Golf (with the family, Hakone) Return home Dinner (restaurant near home)
3	Wed.	1:00 | 4:00 7:00	Meeting (Osaka branch) Dinner (Osaka Hotel)
4	Thu.	10:00 12:00	Meeting (Kyoto branch) Lunch (restaurant in Kyoto)
5	Fri.	12:00 4:00 | 5:00	Lunch (with secretary) Meeting (with Mr. Hayashi, at ABC)
6	Sat.	1:00 7:00	Shopping (with Mrs. Tanaka, department store in Ginza) Dinner (at friend's house)
7	Sun.	9:00 | 11:00 2:00	Tennis (at park, with friends) Tea (at home)

have a meeting, **kaigi o shimasu**, JBP I, p. 6

Lesson 11

Mr. Brown's Life in Tokyo

The pictures show Mr. Brown's daily life in Japan. Make a sentence for each picture.

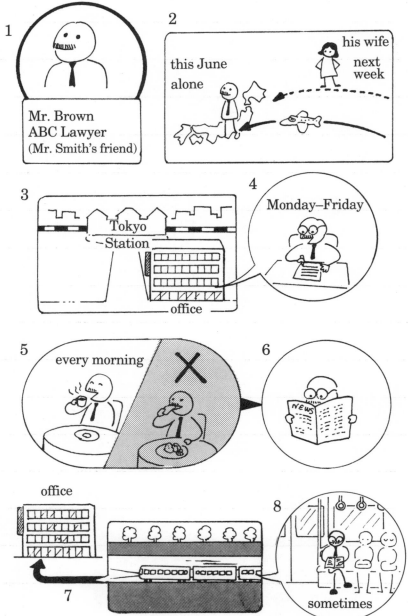

9

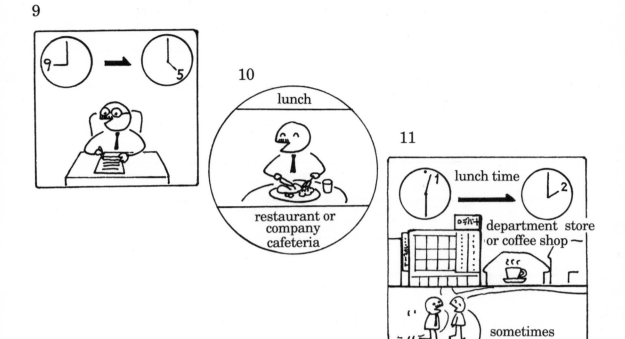

10

lunch

restaurant or
company
cafeteria

11

lunch time

department store
or coffee shop ―

sometimes

12

13

Brown

last night

Smith

Brown

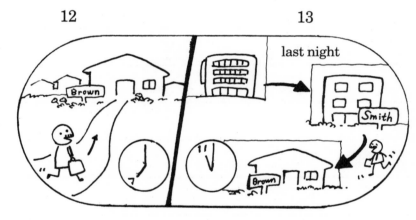

15

Kyoto branch

14

Tokyo

tomorrow

Kyoto

16 Friday

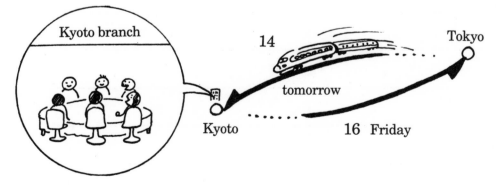

Lesson 12–1

Writing Letters and Telephoning

Describe what Mr. Bijī is doing in picture A as regards the people/places in pictures 1 through 6, and then what he is doing in picture B.

Lesson 12–2

Frequency

Describe what Mr. Bijī is doing in each picture.

1

not often

2

not at all

3

Ginza

with Mariko

often

4

sometimes

with Mr. Satō

5

often

with Mariko

6

not often

Lesson 12–3

Asking for Telephone Numbers

1. Describe what Mr. Satō and Mariko did.

2. Describe what Mr. Kondō and Mariko did.

Lesson 13–1

Adjectives

Memorize the following adjectives.

1 big
2 small
3 good
4 bad
5 ¥1,000
6 ¥50
7
8
9
10
11
12
13 interesting
14 boring
15 delicious

16 *schedule*

17 *schedule*

18 lively

19 quiet

20 famous

21 kind, helpful

22 healthy

23 Supermarket 24 hours

24 pretty

Lesson 13–2

At a Friend's House

You are visiting a friend. Compliment her on the following.

1 big house

2 near the station, convenient

3 interesting

4 very old

5 delicious

6 beautiful

Lesson 13–3

Offering Tea

Your friend offers you some tea. Make up a suitable dialogue.

Lesson 14

Antonyms

Mr. Sad describes how yesterday's movie, Japanese lesson, dinner, and party were, then Mr. Happy describes the same things.

1 Eiga wa . .   Mr. Sad   Mr. Happy   5

2 Nihongo no *ressun wa . . .   6

3 Ban-gohan wa . .   7

4 Pātī wa . . .   8

ressun, lesson

Lesson 15–1

Giving and Receiving (1)

Describe Mr. Satō's action, followed by Mariko's action.

Lessen 15–2

Giving and Receiving (2)

Make sentences using "give," followed by sentences using "receive."

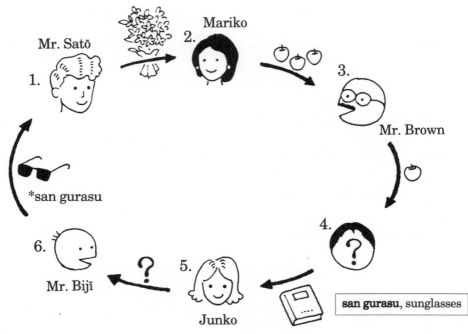

san gurasu, sunglasses

Lesson 15–3

Giving and Receiving (3)

1. Describe what Mr. Satō did, followed by what Mariko did.
2. Make up as many questions and answers as possible.

*St. Valentine's Day, **Barentain dei**

79

Lesson 16–1

Invitation (1)

Mr. Bijī is inviting Mariko to go for a drive. Make up a suitable dialogue.

Lesson 16–2

Invitation (2)

Mr. Bijī is inviting Mariko to dinner. Make up a suitable dialogue.

Lesson 16–3

Refusing an Invitation

Mr. Bijī is inviting Junko to dinner. She is busy and declines but finally accepts.

Lesson 17

Offering to Do Something

Mr. Tanaka is feeling unwell, and Mr. Bijī offers to do various things to make him feel better.

Dō shimashita ka, What's the matter? JBP I, p. 180

eakon, air conditioner

Lesson 18–1

Mr. Bijī's Possessions

Describe what Mr. Bijī has.

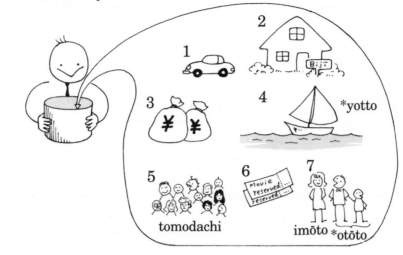

3 ¥ ¥

4 *yotto

5 tomodachi

6 Movie reserved reserved

7 imōto *otōto

> **yotto**, yacht
> **otōto**, younger brother, JBP I, p. 169

Lesson 18–2

Mr. Hoffman's Family

How many sons and daughters does Mr. Hoffman have, and what are their ages?

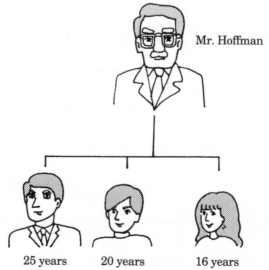

Mr. Hoffman

25 years   20 years   16 years

Lesson 18–3

Time and Place

Give the time or date and the place of each of the following events.

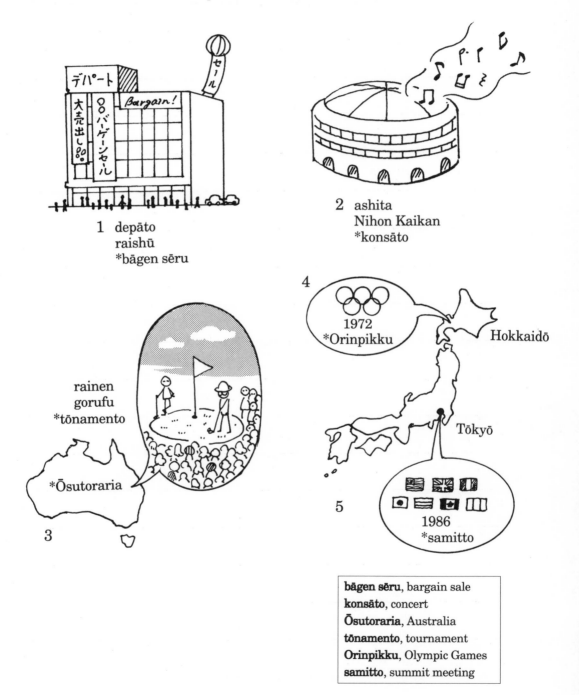

1 depāto
raishū
*bāgen sēru

2 ashita
Nihon Kaikan
*konsāto

rainen
gorufu
*tōnamento

*Ōsutoraria

3

4 1972
*Orinpikku

Hokkaidō

Tōkyō

5 1986
*samitto

bāgen sēru, bargain sale
konsāto, concert
Ōsutoraria, Australia
tōnamento, tournament
Orinpikku, Olympic Games
samitto, summit meeting

Lesson 18–4

Mr. Tanaka's Schedule (3)

Describe Mr. Tanaka's schedule for the coming week.

1	Mon.	9:00–11:00 12:00 4:00	Meeting (office) Lunch (Tokyo Hotel, with Mr. Smith) Meeting (London Securities, Tokyo branch)
2	Tue.	 7:00 5:00 8:00–10:00	**Hakone** Golf (Hakone Golf Club) Telephone office Dinner (restaurant near the golf club)
3	Wed.	 1:00–2:00 4:00 7:00–8:30 9:00	**Osaka** Meeting (Osaka branch) Visit Osaka *factory Dinner (Osaka Hotel) Party (Osaka Club)
4	Thu.	 10:00–11:30 12:00 6:00	**Kyoto** Meeting (Kyoto branch) Lunch (restaurant in Kyoto) Farewell party for Mr. Yamada
5	Fri.	12:00 4:00 6:00	Lunch (with secretary) Meet Mr. Hayashi (at ABC) Party (American Embassy)
6	Sat.	 1:00 6:00–8:00	**Ginza** Shopping Concert (Ginza Hall)
7	Sun.	9:00–11:00 2:00	Tennis (with friends, park) Party (at home) Wedding reception (Kyoto Hotel)

kōjō, factory

Lesson 19–1

A Day in Mr. Bijī's Life

Describe Mr. Bijī's day from the morning on.

Lesson 19–2

The -te Form

Use the **-te** form of the verbs for the actions in the pictures.

Lesson 19–3

Before and After

Describe the following series of actions, using "before" and "after."

Before   After

*repōto

repōto, report

Lessen 19–4

Itineraries

1. Your friend, Linda, has just arrived in Japan. Describe her itinerary as shown below.

SUN	MON	TUE	WED	THU	FRI	SAT
	1	2	3	4	5	6
			Arrived in Japan	Tokyo, 3 days (work) →		◄
7	8	9	10	11	12	13
	Nara, 5 days, with Mrs. Smith (visiting old temples, gardens, etc.) →			◄ Osaka (meet a friend) →		Return to U.S.A.

2. Make your own itinerary. Where would you like to go, and for how long?

SUN	MON	TUE	WED	THU	FRI	SAT
	1	2	3	4	5	6
7	8	9	10	11	12	13

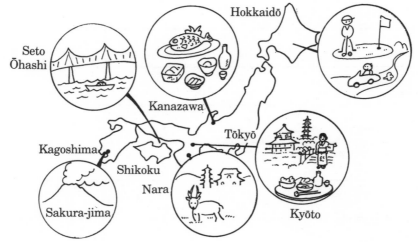

Lesson 20–1

At a Restaurant (1)

You are at a restaurant. Ask for the following items.

1

2

3

4

5

*o-kanjō

o-kanjō, bill

Lesson 20–2

At a Restaurant (2)

1. You are at a restaurant. Order items 1 through 6.
2. Order items 1 and 2.
3. Order items 3 and 4.
4. Order items 2, 3, 5, and 6. You want item 2 to come later.

1

2

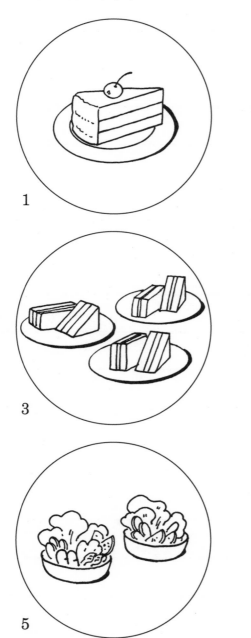

3

4

5

6

Lesson 20–3

Having Things Delivered (1)

You would like to have the following items delivered.

black

blue

red

* kusshion

next Sunday

big

black

white

*hon-bako

* denki sutando

bookcase, **hon-bako**
desk lamp, **denki sutando**
cushion, **kusshion**

Lesson 20–4

Having Things Delivered (2)

Call a *pizza parlor and place the order shown. Ask for the order to be delivered *as quickly as possible.

pizza, **piza**
as quickly as possible, **dekirudake hayaku**

106

Lesson 20–5

Having Things Delivered (3)

Order items 1 through 5 and say by what time you want them delivered.

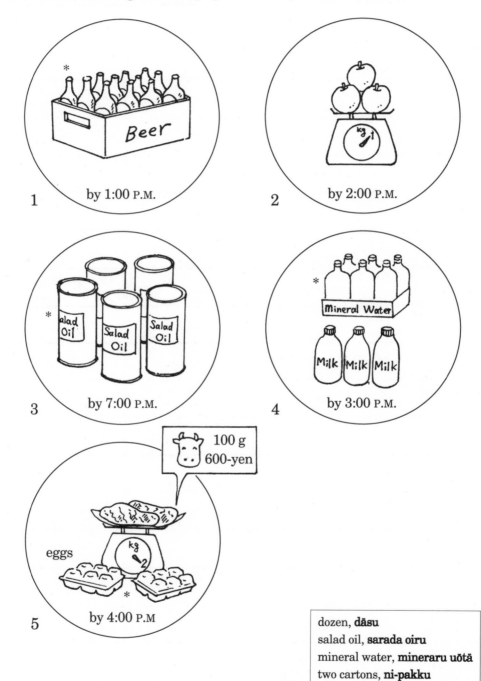

1 by 1:00 P.M.

2 by 2:00 P.M.

3 by 7:00 P.M.

4 by 3:00 P.M.

5 by 4:00 P.M

100 g
600-yen

eggs

dozen, **dāsu**
salad oil, **sarada oiru**
mineral water, **mineraru uōtā**
two cartons, **ni-pakku**

Lesson 21–1

Giving Directions (1)

Memorize the words for 1, 2, and 3.

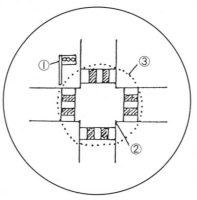

Lesson 21–2

Giving Directions (2)

You are in a taxi. Instruct the driver to go in the direction shown by each arrow and to stop at the places marked with an "x."

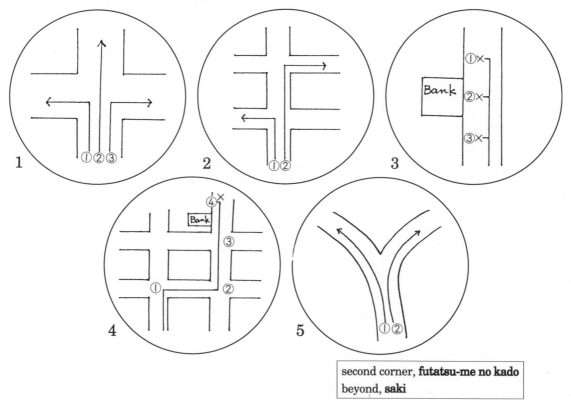

second corner, **futatsu-me no kado**
beyond, **saki**

Lesson 22–1

Transportation (1)

Describe what is happening in each picture, paying attention to the particle.

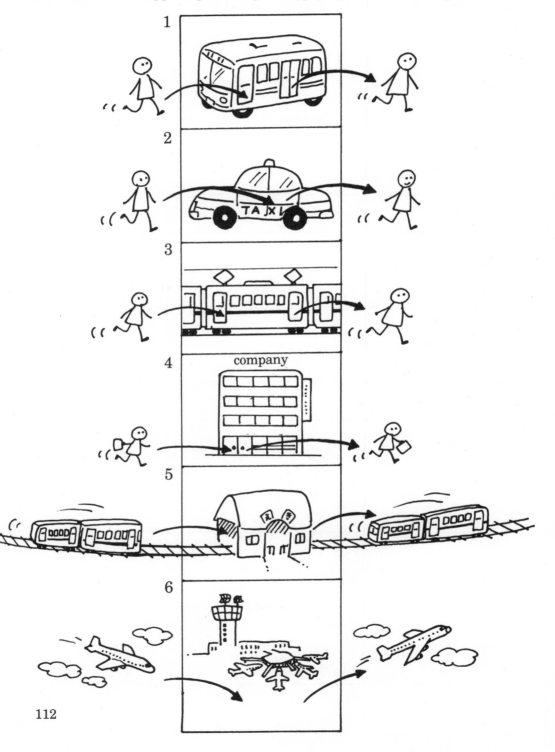

1

2

3

4 company

5

6

Lesson 22–2

Transportation (2)

Describe how to get between the places in each picture, and then say how long it takes.

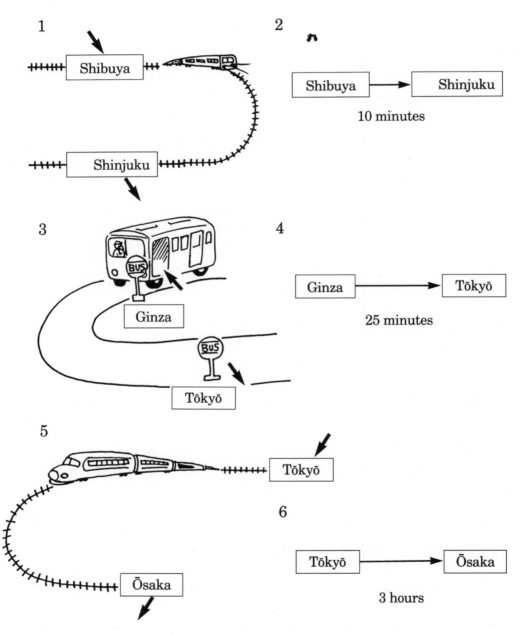

1

Shibuya

Shinjuku

2

Shibuya → Shinjuku

10 minutes

3

Ginza

Tōkyō

4

Ginza → Tōkyō

25 minutes

5

Tōkyō

Ōsaka

6

Tōkyō ⟶ Ōsaka

3 hours

Lesson 22–3

Transportation (3)

Student A should ask Student B how to get to each of the following places from Ogikubo, and then how long it takes.

1. Ginza   2. Ōtemachi   3. Roppongi   4. Asakusa

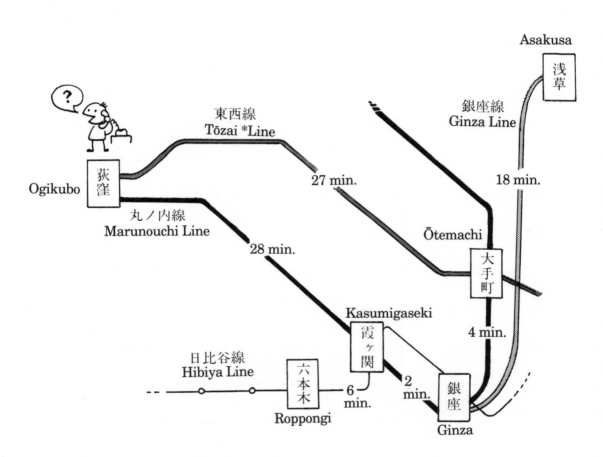

| line, **sen** |
| transfer, **norikaemasu** |

Lesson 23–1

Asking Permission (1)

You are at a friend's house. Ask her permission to do the following.

Lesson 23–2

Asking Permission (2)

Student A is at a company and asks the secretary for permission to do the following things. Student B should answer the requests, and if the answer is negative, the expression of indirect refusal (**sumimasen ga, sore wa chotto. . .** , JBP I, p. 155) should be used.

smoke, **suimasu**, JBP I, p. 155

Lesson 23–3

Asking Permission (3)

1. At the bank, Mr. Bijī is asked to write down his name and address, but he has no pen and asks if he can use one on the desk. Make up a suitable dialogue.

2. Mr. Bijī asks if he may call Mariko tomorrow.

Lesson 23-4

Asking Permission (4)

At a Christmas party, you admire the following things and ask your friend for permission to do what is suggested by the items.

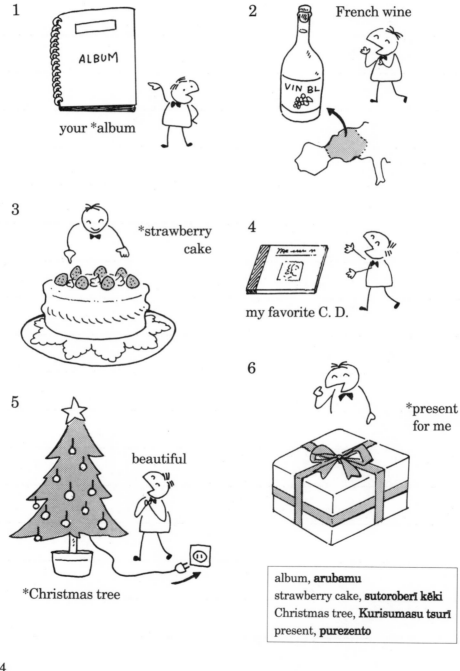

1   your *album

2   French wine

3   *strawberry cake

4   my favorite C. D.

5   beautiful   *Christmas tree

6   *present for me

album, **arubamu**
strawberry cake, **sutoroberī kēki**
Christmas tree, **Kurisumasu tsurī**
present, **purezento**

Lesson 24–1

Negative Requests (1)

What would you say to prevent someone from doing the following?

Lesson 24–2

Negative Requests (2)

What would you say to prevent someone from doing the following?

*trash can

*garbage

trash can, **gomi-bako**
garbage, **gomi**
throw away, **sutemasu**
stand, **tachimasu**
push, **oshimasu**, JBP I, p. 130
step on, **fumimasu**
laugh at, **waraimasu**
get angry, **okorimasu**
cry, **nakimasu**

Lesson 24–3

Refusing a Request

Student A is at his friend's house and asks permission to do the following actions. Student B politely declines, giving a reason. Think of original reasons.

Lesson 25–1

Tenses (1)

Describe the action shown in each picture, paying attention to the tense.

clean, **sōji o shimasu**
cut, **kirimasu**

Lesson 25–2

Tenses (2)

Describe what each person is doing.

1 Mr. Katō
2 Mr. Suzuki
3 Mr. Nakamura
5 Yoshiko, copying
4 Mr. Itō, waiting

6 Mr. Watanabe
7 Mr. Tanaka
8 Mr. Kondō
9 Mr. Hayashi, explaining

10 Mr. Yoshida
11 Ms. Harada
12 Mr. Satō
13 Mr. Sasaki
14 Mr. Anderson
15 Mariko
16 Ms. Yamada

Hello.·····

* sleep, **nemasu**

Lesson 26

At a Party

Mr. Suzuki invites Mr. Brown to a party. Make up suitable conversations.

Lesson 27–1

Tenses (3)

Make sentences for the pictures, paying attention to the tense.

wear a tie, **nekutai o shimasu**
wear/put on, **kimasu**

Lesson 27–2

The Hoffmans

Describe the occupations of the members of the Hoffman family, where they live, and their marital status.

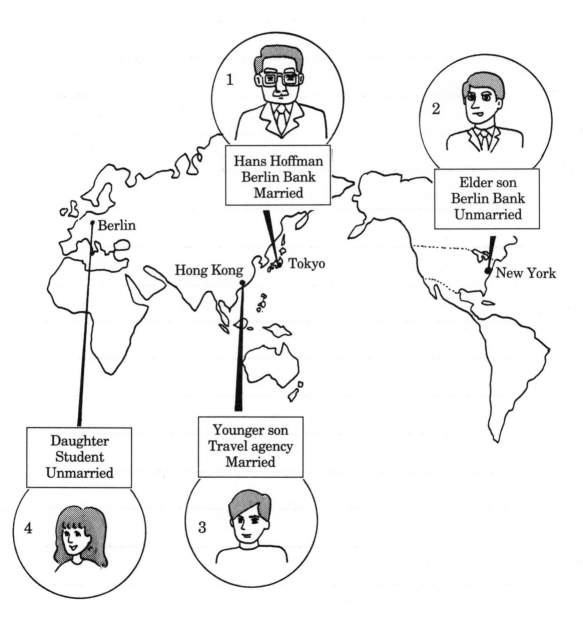

Hans Hoffman
Berlin Bank
Married

Elder son
Berlin Bank
Unmarried

Berlin

Hong Kong   Tokyo

New York

Daughter
Student
Unmarried

Younger son
Travel agency
Married

Lesson 27–3

Various Schedules

Describe the following people's schedules.

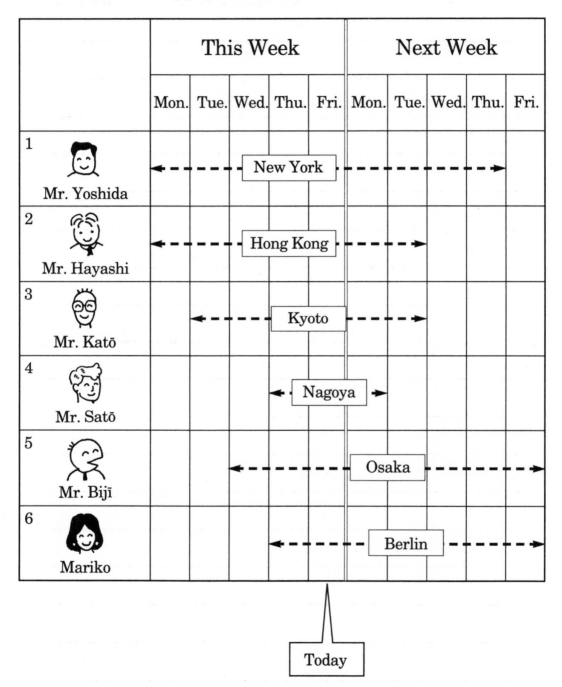

	This Week					Next Week				
	Mon.	Tue.	Wed.	Thu.	Fri.	Mon.	Tue.	Wed.	Thu.	Fri.
1 Mr. Yoshida	←			New York					→	
2 Mr. Hayashi	←			Hong Kong			→			
3 Mr. Katō		←		Kyoto		→				
4 Mr. Satō				← Nagoya →						
5 Mr. Bijī			←		Osaka					→
6 Mariko				←		Berlin				→

Today

Lesson 27–4

People's Profiles

Describe where the following people live, which company they work for, and what kind of person they are.

1	2	3
Mr. Satō Shinjuku Tokyo Electric enjoyable	Mr. Bijī Aoyama New York Securities busy	Mariko Ginza New York Securities kind
4	5	6
Mr. Fukuda Azabu Berlin Bank cheerful	Ms. Kanda Yokohama Tokyo Electric *serious	Junko Akasaka Tokyo Electric lively

serious, **majime (na)**

Lesson 28–1

Hobbies

Describe what each person likes, is good at, and a language they can speak.

| Mr. Satō | Mr. Bijī | Junko | Mariko |

*song

song, **uta**

Lesson 28-2

Desires

Describe what you would like to do.

Lesson 28-3

Feeling Sick

Make up a suitable dialogue.

Lesson 29

Reading a Menu

You are at a restaurant with some friends.
Discuss what to order with your friends.

メニュー

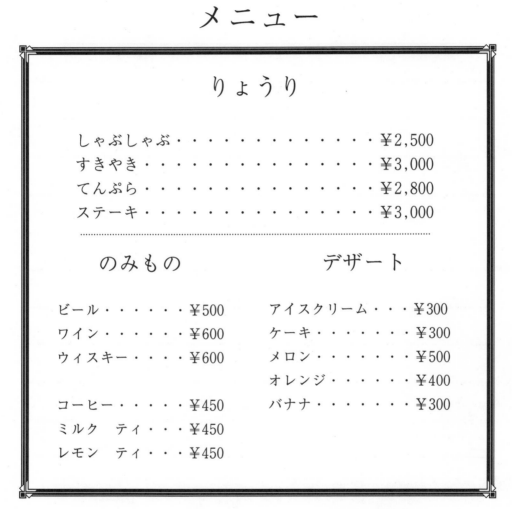

りょうり

しゃぶしゃぶ・・・・・・・・・・・・・	￥2,500
すきやき・・・・・・・・・・・・・・	￥3,000
てんぷら・・・・・・・・・・・・・・	￥2,800
ステーキ・・・・・・・・・・・・・・	￥3,000

のみもの

ビール・・・・・・	￥500
ワイン・・・・・・	￥600
ウィスキー・・・・	￥600
コーヒー・・・・・	￥450
ミルク　ティ・・・	￥450
レモン　ティ・・・	￥450

デザート

アイスクリーム・・・	￥300
ケーキ・・・・・・・	￥300
メロン・・・・・・・	￥500
オレンジ・・・・・・	￥400
バナナ・・・・・・・	￥300

Lesson 30

On a Train

You are on a Shinkansen train bound for Kyoto. Traveling by yourself. You are bored and the man sitting next to you seems bored, too, so you start a conversation.

1   Address the man next to you and tell him what you are going to do in Kyoto.

2   Ask which temples, hotels, and restaurants he recommends.

3   Tell him where you work, what your job is, and where you live.

4   Describe what you do every day and what you are interested in.

5   Invite him to have a meal with you in the *dining car.

6   When you arrive in Kyoto, thank him and leave.

dining car : **shokudō-sha**

152

Verbs

Words with asterisks are words not included in *Japanese for Busy People I*.
The numbers indicate the pages in *Japanese for Busy People I* on which the
words are discussed.

arrive	tsukimasu	146
ask	kikimasu	90
be [for inanimate things]	arimasu	20
be [for living things]	imasu	66
be [for person, polite form]	irasshaimasu	61
be able to	dekimasu	143
be careful	ki o tsukemasu	166
be crowded	konde imasu, komimasu	189
be different	chigaimasu	92
be done	dekimasu	143
be employed	tsutomete imasu	168
be finished	dekimasu	174
be ready	dekimasu	174
be wrong	chigaimasu	92
beg a favor	onegai shimasu	88
bring	mottekimasu	137
build	tsukurimasu	189
buy	kaimasu	79
call (telephone)	denwa o shimasu	79
call	yobimasu	130
can (do)	dekimasu	143
change, transfer	* norikaemasu	
clean	* sōji o shimasu	
close	shimemasu	121
come	kimasu	56
come	irasshaimasu	61
come back	kaerimasu	53
cost	kakarimasu	145
cry	* nakimasu	

156

play tennis	tenisu o shimasu	108
push	oshimasu	130
put, leave	* okimasu	
put on a tie	nekutai o shimasu	110
read	yomimasu	79
receive	moraimasu	108
receive [polite-humble]	itadakimasu	95
return	kaerimasu	53
ride	norimasu	145
say	iimasu	137
see	mimasu	78
see (meet a person)	aimasu	89
sell	utte imasu, urimasu	170
send	okurimasu	178
shop	kaimono o shimasu	81
show	misemasu	39
shut	shimemasu	121
sit down	kakemasu	61
ski	sukī o shimasu	114
sleep	* nemasu	
smoke	suimasu	155
stand	* tachimasu	
stay	imasu	130
step on	* fumimasu	
stop, park	tomemasu	138
study	benkyō o shimasu	80
switch off	keshimasu	121
switch on	tsukemasu	121
take (of time)	kakarimasu	145
take (a picture)	torimasu	150
take (a taxi, etc.)	norimasu	145
take a trip	ryokō o shimasu	129
take a walk	sampo o shimasu	116
talk	hanashi o shimasu	161
teach	oshiemasu	90
telephone	denwa o shimasu	79
tell	oshiemasu	90
throw away	* sutemasu	
transfer (change)	* norikaemasu	
turn	magarimasu	138
turn on	tsukemasu	121
type	taipu o shimasu	89
understand	wakarimasu	104
use	tsukaimasu	150
wait	machimasu	92
walk	arukimasu	145
watch	mimasu	78
wear	* kimasu	

Adjectives

a few	* sukunai		kind	shinsetsuna	100
a little	* sukunai		large	ōkii	49
bad	warui	97	late	osoi	166
black	kuroi	50	light (in weight)	* karui	
blue	aoi	50	lively	nigiyakana	99
boring	tsumaranai	98	long	* nagai	
bright	* akarui		low	* hikui	
brown	* chairoi		many	* ōi	
busy	isogashii	100	much	* ōi	
cheap	yasui	100	narrow	* semai	
clean	kireina	95	near	chikai	98
cold	samui	104	new	atarashii	100
convenient	benrina	100	no good	damena	155
cool	* suzushii		old	furui	100
correct	* tadashii		painful	itai	176
dark	kurai	121	purple	* murasaki (no)	
dangerous	* abunai		pretty	kireina	95
delicious	oishii	95	quiet	shizukana	97
difficult	muzukashii	100	red	akai	49
dislike	* kiraina		rude	shitsureina	61
early	* hayai		safe	* anzenna	
easy	yasashii	100	salty	* shiokarai	
enjoyable	tanoshii	106	serious	* majimena	
expensive	takai	100	short	* mijikai	
famous	yūmeina	95	skillful	jōzuna	176
far	tōi	97	slow	osoi	166
fast	* hayai		spicy	* karai	
favorite	sukina	109	sour	* suppai	
good	ii	79	sweet	* amai	
green	aoi (midori no)	50	unkind	* fu-shinsetsuna	
healthy	genkina	100	unskillful	* hetana	
heavy	* omoi		various	iroirona	174
high	* takai		warm	* atatakai	
hot	atsui	104	well	genkina	100
important	* daijina		white	* shiroi	
inconvenient	* fubenna		wide	* hiroi	
interesting	omoshiroi	100	yellow	* kiiroi	

Answer Section

Sentences will sound natural if each word or phrase marked off by / is pronounced smoothly and given equal emphasis.

L1–1
1. Nihon   2. Chū/goku   3. Doi/tsu   4. Igi/risu   5. Fura/nsu   6. Ame/rika
7. Nihon/-jin   8. Chū/goku/-jin   9. Doi/tsu/-jin   10. Igi/risu/-jin
11. Fura/nsu/-jin   12. Ame/rika/-jin

L1–2
1. Hayashi-san.   Kochira wa / Tōkyō / Denki no / Tanaka-san / desu.
2. Hayashi-san.   Kochira wa / Berurin / Ginkō no / Hofuman-san / desu.
3. Hayashi-san.   Kochira wa / Furansu / Taishikan no / Dyupon-san / desu.
4. Hayashi-san.   Kochira wa / Rondon / Shōken no / Buraun-san / desu.
5. Hayashi-san.   Kochira wa / Berurin / Ginkō no / Suzuki-san / desu. Suzuki-san wa / hisho desu.
6. Hayashi-san.   Kochira wa / ABC no / Sumisu-san / desu. Sumisu-san wa / bengoshi / desu.
7. Hayashi-san.   Kochira wa / Tōkyō / Daigaku no / Rin-san / desu. Rin-san wa / gakusei / desu.

L2
1. Buraun-san no/kaisha no/denwa-bangō wa/zero san no/san yon yon yon no/yon ni ni san/desu.
Uchi no/denwa-bangō wa/zero san no/san yon yon go no/go yon go yon/desu.
2. Dyupon-san no/taishikan no/denwa bangō wa/zero san no/san ichi ichi san no/ichi ichi ichi ni/desu.
Uchi no/denwa-bangō wa/zero san no/san ni ni san no/ichi ichi ichi san/desu.
3. Sumisu-san no/kaisha no/denwa bangō wa/zero san no/san roku roku go no/ichi ichi roku roku/desu.
Uchi no/denwa-bangō wa/zero san no/san roku roku ni no/ni roku roku nana/desu.
4. Suzuki-san no/ginkō no/denwa bangō wa/zero san no/san yon kyū yon no/ichi ichi ichi go/desu.

Uchi no/denwa-bangō wa/zero san no/san hachi hachi nana no/roku hachi roku hachi/desu.

5. Rin-san no/uchi no/denwa-bangō wa/zero san no/san nana hachi hachi no/kyū hachi kyū hachi/desu.

6. Tanaka-san no/kaisha no/denwa bangō wa/zero san no/san kyū ni kyū no/ichi kyū kyū kyū/desu.

Uchi no/denwa-bangō wa/zero san no/san ichi hachi kyū no/nana ni kyū nana desu.

L3–1

1. Go-ji/desu.
2. Hachi-ji/desu.
3. Jū/ichi-ji/desu
4. Jū/ni-ji/desu.
5. Shichi-ji/desu.
6. Roku-ji/desu.
7. Ni-ji/desu.
8. Yo-ji/desu.
9. Jū-ji/desu.
10. San-ji/desu.
11. Ichi-ji/desu.
12. Ku-ji/desu.
13. Depāto wa/ku-ji kara/shichi-ji made/desu.
14. Ginkō wa/ku-ji kara/san-ji made/desu.
15. Yūbin/kyoku wa/ku-ji kara/go-ji made/desu.
16. Eiga wa/yo-ji kara/roku-ji han/made/desu.

L3–2

1. Shigoto wa/ku-ji kara/go-ji made/desu.
2. Hiru-yasumi wa/jūni-ji kara/ichi-ji made/desu.
3. Kaigi wa/ni-ji kara/yo-ji han/made desu.
4. Pātī wa/go-ji han/kara desu.

L3-3

1. Suzuki-san no/tanjōbi wa/tsuitachi/desu.
2. Natsu-yasumi wa/futsuka kara/tōka made/desu.
3. Shutchō wa/jūgo-nichi kara/jūku-nichi made/desu.
4. Hayashi-san no/tanjōbi wa/hatsuka desu.
5. Gorufu wa/nijū/yokka desu.

L4

1. Shimbun wa/hyaku/yonjū-/en desu.
2. Ringo wa/sanbyaku-/en desu.
3. Hon wa/roppyaku-/en desu.
4. Kasa wa/sanzen-/en desu.
5. Rajio wa/gosen/sanbyaku-/en desu.
6. Tēpurekōdā wa/gosen/roppyaku-/en desu.
7. Tokei wa/sanman/gosen/roppyaku-/en desu.
8. Terebi wa/sanman/hassen/happyaku-/en desu.
9. Nihon no/kuruma wa/sanbyaku/kyūjūman-/en desu.
10. Doitsu no/kuruma wa/happyakuman-/en desu.
11. Uchi wa/ichioku/sanzen/sanbyakuman-/en desu.

L5

1. Akai/kasa o/kudasai.
2. Aoi/kasa o/kudasai.
3. Ōkii/ringo o/kudasai.
4. Chiisai/ringo o/kudasai.

5. Furansu no/sētā o/kudasai.   6. Igirisu no/sētā o/kudasai.
7. Rokujū/ni-en no/kitte o/kudasai.   8. Yonjū/ichi-en no/kitte o/kudasai.
9. Ōkii/ringo o/mittsu/kudasai.   10. Chiisai/ringo o/futatsu/kudasai.
11. Yonjū/ichi-en no/kitte o/ni-mai/kudasai.
12. Rokujū/ni-en no/kitte o/go-mai/kudasai.

L6–1

1. ginkō   2. Fuji-san   3. Furansu   4. Furansu/shisha   5. Ginza no/depāto
6. tomodachi no/uchi   7. Tōkyō/eki   8. Bijī-san no/uchi

L6–2

1. Bijī-san wa/ashita/ginkō ni/ikimasu.
2. (Bijī-san wa)/ashita/Fuji-san ni/ikimasu.
3. (Bijī-san wa)/ashita/Furansu ni/ikimasu.
4. (Bijī-san wa)/ashita/Furansu/shisha ni/ikimasu.
5. (Bijī-san wa)/kinō/Ginza no/depāto ni/ikimashita.
6. (Bijī-san wa)/kinō/tomodachi no/uchi ni/ikimashita.
7. (Bijī-san wa)/kinō/Tōkyō/eki ni/ikimashita.
8. (Bijī-san wa)/kinō/doko ni/ikimashita ka.
9. (Bijī-san wa)/kinō/uchi ni/kaerimashita.

L6–3

1. Bijī-san wa/ashita/Buraun-san to/ginkō ni/ikimasu.
2. (Bijī-san wa)/ashita/Satō-san to/Fuji-san ni/ikimasu.
3. (Bijī-san wa)/ashita (hitori de) Furansu ni/ikimasu.
4. (Bijī-san wa)/ashita/Kondō-san to/Furansu/shisha ni/ikimasu.
5. (Bijī-san wa)/kinō/tomodachi to/Ginza no/depāto ni/ikimashita.
6. (Bijī-san wa)/kinō (hitori de) tomodachi no/uchi ni/ikimashita.
7. (Bijī-san wa)/kinō/dare to/Tōkyō/eki ni/ikimashita ka.
8. (Bijī-san wa)/kinō/doko ni/ikimashita ka.
9. (Bijī-san wa)/kinō/uchi ni/kaerimashita.

L6-4

1. A: Bijī-san wa/doko ni/ikimasu ka.
   B: Ginkō ni/ikimasu.
   A: Itsu/ikimasu ka.
   B: Ashita/ikimasu.
   A: Dare to/ikimasu ka
   B: Buraun-san to/ikimasu.
2. A: Bijī-san wa/doko ni/ikimasu ka.
   B: Fujisan ni/ikimasu.
   A: Itsu/ikimasu ka.
   B: Ashita/ikimasu.
   A: Dare to/ikimasu ka.
   B: Satō-san to/ikimasu.
3. A: Bijī-san wa/doko ni/ikimasu ka.
   B: Furansu ni/ikimasu.
   A: Itsu/ikimasu ka.

B: Ashita/ikimasu.
A: Dare to/ikimasu ka.
B: Hitori de/ikimasu.
4. A: Bijī-san wa/dokoni/ikimasu ka.
B: Furansu/shisha ni/ikimasu.
A: Itsu/ikimasu ka.
B: Ashita/ikimasu.
A: Dare to/ikimasu ka.
B: Kondō-san to/ikimasu.
5. A: Bijī-san wa/doko ni/ikimashita ka.
B: Ginza no/depāto ni/ikimashita.
A: Itsu/ikimashita ka.
B: Kinō/ikimashita.
A: Dare to/ikimashita ka.
B: Tomodachi to/ikimashita.
6. A: Bijī-san wa/doko ni/ikimashita ka.
B: Tomodachi no/uchi ni/ikimashita.
A: Itsu/ikimashita ka.
B: Kinō/ikimashita.
A: Dare to/ikimashita ka.
B: Hitori de/ikimashita.

L6–5
1. Kono basu wa/Ginza ni/ikimasu ka.
2. Iie, ikimasen.
3. Dono/basu ga/ikimasu ka.
4. Ano/hachijū/ni-ban no/basu ga/ikimasu.
5. Arigatō/gozaimashita.

L7–1
1. Bijī-san wa/raishū/takushī de/ginkō ni/ikimasu.
2. (Bijī-san wa)/kyonen/basu de/Fuji-san ni/ikimashita.
3. (Bijī-san wa) sen/kyūhyaku/hachijū/kyū-nen ni/hikōki de Furansu ni/ikimashita.
4. (Bijī-san wa) sengetsu/hikōki de/Furansu/shisha ni/ikimashita.
5. (Bijī-san wa) senshū no/do-yōbi ni/densha de/Ginza no/depāto ni/iki mashita.
6. (Bijī-san wa) ashita no/yo-ji ni/aruite/tomodachi no/uchi ni/ikimasu.
7. (Bijī-san wa) kinō no/roku-ji ni/Buraun-san to/kuruma de/Tōkyō/eki ni/ikimashita.
8. (Bijī-san wa) kinō/Satō-san to/kuruma de/doko ni/ikimashita ka.
9. (Bijī-san wa) ashita/nan de/uchi ni/kaerimasu ka.

L7–2
1. Tanaka-san wa/getsu-yōbi no/jūni-ji ni/takushī de/Sumisu-san to/Tōkyō/Hoteru ni/ikimasu.
   Yo-ji ni/takushī de/Rondon/Shōken no/Tōkyō/shisha ni/ikimasu.
2. Ka-yōbi wa/yasumi desu.

Kuruma de/kazoku to/Hakone ni/ikimasu.
Shichi-ji ni/uchi ni/kaerimasu.
3. Sui-yōbi ni/hikōki de/hitori de/Ōsaka/shisha ni/ikimasu.
4. Moku-yōbi ni/Ōsaka/shisha no/hito to Kyōto/shisha ni/ikimasu.
Shinkansen de/Tōkyō ni/kaerimasu.
5. Kin-yōbi no/jūni-ji ni/hisho to/resutoran ni/ikimasu.
Yo-ji ni/Hayashi-san to/ABC ni/ikimasu.
Roku-ji ni/Amerika/Taishikan ni/ikimasu.
6. Do-yōbi no/ichi-ji ni/okusan to/depāto ni/ikimasu.
Shichi-ji ni/okusan to/tomodachi no/uchi ni/ikimasu.
7. Nichi-yōbi no/ku-ji ni/tomodachi to/kōen ni/ikimasu.
Ni-ji ni/tomodachi ga/Tanaka-san no/uchi ni/kimasu.

L8–1

1. Ikkai ni/Hofuman-san ga/imasu.
2. Nikai ni/Sumisu-san ga/imasu.
3. Sangai ni/Tanaka-san ga/imasu.
4. Yonkai ni/dare mo/imasen.
5. Gokai ni/dare ga/imasu ka.
6. Ikkai ni/ginkō ga/arimasu.
7. Nikai ni/ABC ga/arimasu.
8. Sangai ni/Tōkyō/Denki ga/arimasu.
9. Yonkai ni/nani mo/arimasen.
10. Gokai ni/nani ga/arimasu ka.

L8–2

Shokudō ga/arimasu.   Shokudō no/hidari ni/ima ga/arimasu.
Ima no/hidari ni/genkan ga/arimasu.   Shokudō no/migi ni/daidokoro
ga/arimasu. Daidokoro no/migi ni/furoba ga/arimasu.   Shokudō ni/tana
to/tēburu ga/arimasu.   Ima ni/terebi to/sofā ga/arimasu.   Genkan ni/e
ga/arimasu.Daidokoro ni/reizōko ga/arimasu.   Furoba ni/kansōki to/sentakuki
ga/arimasu.

L9–1

1. Niwa ni/tēburu ga/mittsu/arimasu.
2. Niwa ni/isu ga/tō/arimasu.
3. Niwa ni/onna no ko ga/hitori to/otoko no ko ga/futari to//imasu.
4. Daidokoro ni/ringo ga/kokonotsu/arimasu.
5. Ima ni/kaban ga/mittsu/arimasu.
6. Ima ni/tēburu ga/hitotsu/arimasu.

L9–2

1. Kagi wa/hako no/naka ni/arimasu.
2. Megane wa/terebi no/ue ni/arimasu.
3. Denwa wa/tēburu no/ue ni/arimasu.
4. Kasa wa/tēburu no/shita ni/arimasu.
5. Shimbun wa/isu no/ue ni/arimasu.
6. Haizara wa/isu no/shita ni/arimasu.

7. Bijī-san wa/uchi no/naka ni/imasu.

8. Kuruma wa/uchi no/mae ni/arimasu.

9. Resutoran wa/hoteru no/tonari ni/arimasu.

10. Hon-ya wa/resutoran no/tonari ni/arimasu.

11. Taishikan wa/gokai ni/arimasu.

12. Ginkō wa/yonkai ni/arimasu.

13. Tōkyō Denki wa/sangai ni/arimasu.

14. ABC wa/nikai ni/arimasu.

15. Uketsuke wa/ikkai ni/arimasu.

16. Garēji wa/chika/ikkai ni/arimasu.

L10–1

1. Bijī-san wa/ban-gohan o/tabemasu.

2. (Bijī-san wa)/kōhī o/nomimasu.

3. (Bijī-san wa)/kamera o/kaimasu.

4. (Bijī-san wa)/ongaku o/kikimasu.

5. (Bijī-san wa)/terebi o/mimasu.

6. (Bijī-san wa)/hon o/yomimasu.

7. (Bijī-san wa)/benkyō o/shimasu.

8. (Bijī-san wa)/shigoto o/shimasu.

9. (Bijī-san wa)/tenisu o/shimasu.

L10–2

1. Bijī-san wa/resutoran de/ban-gohan o/tabemasu.

2. (Bijī-san wa)/kissaten de/kōhī o/nomimasu.

3. (Bijī-san wa)/depāto de/kamera o/kaimasu.

4. (Bijī-san wa)/uchi de/ongaku o/kikimasu.

5. (Bijī-san wa)/uchi de terebi o/mimasu.

6. (Bijī-san wa)/ima de/hon o/yomimasu.

7. (Bijī-san wa)/gakkō de/benkyō o/shimasu.

8. (Bijī-san wa)/kaisha de/shigoto o/shimasu.

9. (Bijī-san wa)/tenisu/kurabu de/tenisu o/shimasu.

10. (Bijī-san wa)/kuruma de/Shinjuku ni/ikimasu.

L10–3

1. 1. Bijī-san wa/resutoran de/sutēki to/sarada o/tabemasu.

2. (Bijī-san wa)/bā de/wain ya/uisukī o/nomimasu.

3. (Bijī-san wa)/nichi-yōbi ni/depāto de/kamera o/kaimasu.

4. (Bijī-san wa)/uchi de/tomodachi to/ongaku o/kikimasu.

5. (Bijī-san wa)/hachi-ji kara/jū-ji made/uchi de/terebi o/mimasu.

6. (Bijī-san wa)/nichi-yōbi no/asa/ima de/kuruma no/hon o/yomimasu.

7. (Bijī-san wa)/jū-ji kara/gakkō de/benkyō o/shimasu.

8. (Bijī-san wa)/getsu-yōbi kara/do-yōbi made/kaisha de/shigoto o/shimasu.

9. (Bijī-san wa)/do-yōbi no/san-ji kara/go-ji made/tenisu kurabu de/ tenisu o/shimasu.

10. (Bijī-san wa)/doko de shimbun o/yomimasu ka.

2. 1. A: Bijī-san wa/nani o/tabemasu ka.

B: Sutēki to/sarada o/tabemasu.
A: Doko de/tabemasu ka.
B: Resutoran de/tabemasu.

2. A: Bijī-san wa/nani o/nomimasu ka.
B: Wain ya/uisukī/o nomimasu.
A: Doko de/nomimasu ka.
B: Bā de/nomimasu.

3. A: Bijī-san wa/nani o/kaimasu ka.
B: Kamera o/kaimasu.
A: Doko de/kaimasu ka.
B: Depāto de/kaimasu.
A: Itsu/kaimasu ka.
B: Nichi-yōbi ni/kaimasu.

4. A: Bijī-san wa/nani o/kikimasu ka.
B: Ongaku o/kikimasu.
A: Doko de/kikimasu ka.
B: Uchi de/kikimasu.
A: Dare to/kikimasu ka.
B: Tomodachi to/kikimasu.

5. A: Bijī-san wa/nani o/mimasu ka.
B: Terebi o/mimasu.
A: Doko de/mimasu ka.
B: Uchi de/mimasu.
A: Nan-ji kara/nan-ji made/mimasu ka.
B: Hachi-ji kara/jū-ji made/mimasu.

6. A: Bijī-san wa/nani o/yomimasu ka.
B: Kuruma no/hon o/yomimasu.
A: Doko de/yomimasu ka.
B: Ima de/yomimasu.
A: Itsu/yomimasu ka.
B: Nichi-yōbi no/asa/yomimasu.

7. A: Bijī-san wa/doko de/benkyō o/shimasu ka.
B: Gakkō de/shimasu.
A: Nan-ji kara/shimasu ka.
B: Jū-ji kara/shimasu.

8. A: Bijī-san wa/doko de/shigoto o/shimasu ka.
B: Kaisha de/shimasu.
A: Nan-yōbi kara/nan-yōbi made/shimasu ka.
B: Getsu-yōbi kara/do-yōbi made/shimasu.

9. A: Bijī-san wa/doko de/tenisu o/shimasu ka.
B: Tenisu kurabu de/shimasu.
A: Nan-yōbi ni/shimasu ka.
B: Do-yōbi ni/shimasu.
A: Nan-ji kara/nan-ji made/shimasu ka.
B: San-ji kara/go-ji made/shimasu.

L10–4

Sample answer.

1. Tanaka-san wa/getsu-yōbi no/hachi-ji kara/ku-ji made/kaisha de/kaigi o/shimasu.
Sorekara, jūni-ji ni/Tōkyō/Hoteru de/Sumisu-san to/hiru-gohan o/tabemasu.
Soshite, yo-ji kara/go-ji made/Rondon/Shōken no/Tōkyō/shisha de/kaigi o/shimasu.

2. Ka-yōbi wa/yasumi desu.
Kazoku to/Hakone de/gorufu o/shimasu.
Shichi-ji ni/uchi ni/kaerimasu.
Hachi-ji ni/uchi no/chikaku no/resutoran de/ban-gohan o/tabemasu.

3. Sui-yōbi no/ichi-ji kara/yo-ji made/Ōsaka shisha de/kaigi o/shimasu.
Shichi-ji ni/Ōsaka Hoteru de/ban-gohan o/tabemasu.

4. Moku-yōbi no/jū-ji ni/Kyōto/shisha de/kaigi o/shimasu.
Jūni-ji ni/Kyōto no/resutoran de/hiru-gohan o/tabemasu.

5. Kin-yōbi no/jūni-ji ni/hisho to/hiru-gohan o/tabemasu.
Yo-ji kara/go-ji made/Hayashi-san to/ABC de/kaigi o/shimasu.

6. Do-yōbi no/ichi-ji ni/okusan to/Ginza no/depāto de/kaimono o/shimasu.
Shichi-ji ni/tomodachi no/uchi de/ban-gohan o/tabemasu.

7. Nichi-yōbi no/ku-ji kara/jūichi-ji made/kōen de/tomodachi to/tenisu o/shimasu.
Ni-ji ni/uchi de/o-cha o/nomimasu.

L11

1. Buraun-san wa ABC no bengoshi desu. Soshite Sumisu-san no tomodachi desu.
2. Buraun-san wa kotoshi no roku-gatsu ni hitori de Nihon ni kimashita.
Okusan wa raishū Nihon ni kimasu.
3. Buraun-san no kaisha wa Tōkyō Eki no chikaku ni arimasu.
4. Shigoto wa getsu-yōbi kara kin-yōbi made desu.
5. Buraun-san wa maiasa kōhī o nomimasu ga, nani mo tabemasen.
6. Soshite shimbun o yomimasu.
7. Chikatetsu de kaisha ni ikimasu.
8. Tokidoki chikatetsu de hon ya zasshi o yomimasu.
9. Kaisha wa ku-ji kara go-ji han made desu.
10. Resutoran ya kaisha no shokudō de hiru-gohan o tabemasu.
11. Hiru-yasumi wa jūni-ji han kara ni-ji made desu kara, tokidoki kaisha no hito to depāto ya kissaten ni ikimasu.
12. Uchi ni shichi-ji goro kaerimasu.
13. Kinō wa kaisha kara Sumisu-san no uchi ni ikimashita kara, jūichi-ji goro uchi ni kaerimashita.
14. Buraun-san wa ashita Shinkansen de Kyōto ni ikimasu.
15. Kyōto no shisha de kaigi o shimasu.
16. Soshite kin-yōbi ni Tōkyō ni kaerimasu.

L12–1

A. 1. Bijī-san wa/Kondō-san ni/tegami o/kakimasu.
　 2. (Bijī-san wa/)otōsan ni/tegami o/kakimasu.

3. (Bijī-san wa)/okāsan ni/tegami o/kakimasu.
4. (Bijī-san wa)/dare ni/tegami o/kakimasu ka.
5. (Bijī-san wa)/Tōkyō/Denki ni/tegami o/kakimasu.
6. (Bijī-san wa)/doko ni/tegami o/kakimasu ka.
B. 1. Bijī-san wa/Kondō-san ni/denwa o/shimasu.
2. (Bijī-san wa)/otōsan ni/denwa o/shimasu.
3. (Bijī-san wa)/okāsan/ni/denwa o/shimasu.
4. (Bijī-san wa)/dare ni/denwa o/shimasu ka.
5. (Bijī-san wa)/Tōkyō/Denki ni/denwa o/shimasu.
6. (Bijī-san wa)/doko ni/denwa o/shimasu ka.

L12–2

1. Bijī-san wa/amari/otōsan ni/tegami o/kakimasen.
2. (Bijī-san wa)/zenzen/gorufu o/shimasen.
3. (Bijī-san wa)/yoku/Mariko-san to/Ginza ni/ikimasu.
4. (Bijī-san wa)/tokidoki/Satō-san to/bīru o/nomimasu.
5. (Bijī-san wa)/yoku/Mariko-san to/ban-gohan o/tabemasu.
6. (Bijī-san wa)/amari/zasshi o/yomimasen.

L12–3

1. Satō-san wa/Mariko-san ni/aimashita.
   Soshite, Mariko-san ni/denwa-bangō o/kikimashita.
   Mariko-san wa/Satō-san ni/aimashita.
   Soshite, Satō-san ni/denwa-bangō o/oshiemashita.
2. Kondō-san wa/Mariko-san ni/aimashita.
   Soshite, Mariko-san ni/denwa-bangō o/kikimashita.
   Mariko-san wa/Kondō-san ni/aimashita
   Denwa-bangō o/oshiemasendeshita.

L13–1

1. ō/kii/desu	2. chii/sai/desu	3. ii/desu
4. warui/desu	5. takai/desu	6. yasui/desu
7. furui/desu	8. atara/shii/desu	9. yasa/shii/desu
10. muzuka/shii/desu	11. chikai/desu	12. tōi/desu
13. omoshi/roi/desu	14. tsumara/nai/desu	15. oi/shii/desu
16. isoga/shii/desu	17. hima/desu	18. nigi/yaka/desu
19. shizuka/desu	20. yū/mei/desu	21. shin/setsu/desu
22. genki/desu	23. benri/desu	24. kirei/desu

L13–2

1. Ōkii/uchi desu/ne.
2. Eki kara/chikai desu/ne. Benri desu/ne.
3. Omoshiroi/desu ne.
4. Totemo/furui desu/ne.
5. Oishii/desu.
6. Kirei desu/ne.

L13–3

1. O-cha o dōzo.
2. Arigatō gozaimasu.
3. O-kashi wa ikaga desu ka.
4. Hai, itadakimasu.
5. Kireina o-kashi desu ne.
6. Nihon no o-kashi desu ka.

7. Ee, sō desu.
8. Totemo oishii desu.　　　9. O-cha o mō ippai ikaga desu ka.
10. Iie, mō kekkō desu.

L14

Mr. Sad.
1. Kinō no/eiga wa/omoshiroku/nakatta/desu. (tsumarana/katta/desu)
2. Nihon-go no/ressun wa/muzukashi/katta/desu.
3. Ban-gohan wa/oishiku/nakatta/desu.
4. Pātī wa/tanoshiku/nakatta/desu.

Mr. Happy.
5. Kinō no/eiga wa/omoshiro/katta/desu.
6. Nihon-go no/ressun wa/muzukashiku/nakatta/desu.
   (yasashi/katta/desu)
7. Ban-gohan wa/oishi/katta/desu.　　　8. Pātī wa/tanoshi/katta/desu.

L15–1

1. Satō-san wa/Mariko san ni/hana o/agemasu.
2. Mariko-san wa/Satō san ni/hana o/moraimasu.

L15-2

"give"
1. Satō-san wa/Mariko-san ni/hana o/agemasu.
2. Mariko-san wa/Buraun-san ni/ringo o/mittsu/agemasu.
3. Buraun-san wa/dare ni/ringo o/agemasu ka.
4. Dare ga/Junko-san ni/hon o/agemasu ka.
5. Junko-san wa/Bijī-san ni/nani o/agemasu ka.
6. Bijī-san wa/Satō-san ni/sangurasu o/agemasu.
"receive"
1. Satō-san wa/Bijī-san ni/sangurasu o/moraimasu.
2. Mariko-san wa/Satō-san ni/hana o/moraimasu.
3. Buraun-san wa/Mariko-san ni/ringo o/mittsu/moraimasu.
4. Dare ga/Buraun-san ni/ringo o/moraimasu ka.
5. Junko-san wa/dare ni/hon o/moraimasu ka.
6. Bijī-san wa/Junko-san ni/nani o/moraimasu ka.

L15–3

Christmas
1. Kurisumasu ni/Satō-san wa/Mariko-san ni/goman-en no/tokei o/agemashita.
   Soshite, Mariko-san ni/hassen-en no/san gurasu o/moraimashita.
   Mariko-san wa/Satō-san ni/hassen-en no/san gurasu o/agemashita.
   Soshite, Satō-san ni/goman-en no/tokei o/moraimashita.
2. A: Kurisumasu ni/Satō-san wa/Mariko-san ni/nani o/agemashita ka.
   B: Tokei o/agemashita.
   A: Donna/tokei o/agemashita ka.
   B: Kireina/tokei o/agemashita.
   A: Ikura no/tokei o/agemashita ka.
   B: Goman-en no/tokei o/agemashita.

St. Valentine's Day
1. Barentain-dei ni/Satō-san wa/Mariko-san ni/nisen-roppyaku/-en no/ hana o/agemashita.
Soshite, Mariko-san ni/sen-sanbyaku/-en no/chokorēto o/moraimashita.
Mariko-san wa/Satō-san ni/sen/-sanbyaku/-en no/ chokorēto o/agemashita.
Soshite, Satō-san ni/nisen/-roppyaku/-en no/hana o/moraimashita.
2. A: Barentain-de ni/Satō-san wa/Mariko-san ni/nani o/agemashita ka.
B: Hana o/agemashita.
A: Donna/hana o/agemashita.
B: Kireina/hana o/agemashita.
A: Ikura no/hana o/agemashita ka.
B: Nisen/-roppyaku/-en no/hana o/agemashita.

Birthday
1. Tanjōbi ni/Satō-san wa/Mariko-san ni/e to/hon to/kutsu o/agemashita.
Soshite, Mariko-san ni/Fransu no kasa o/moraimashita.
Mariko-san wa/Satō-san ni/Furansu no/kasa o/agemashita.
Soshite, Satō-san ni/e to/hon to/kutsu o/moraimashita.
2. A: Tanjōbi ni/Satō-san wa/Mariko-san ni/nani o/agemashita ka.
B: E to/hon to/kutsu o/agemashita.
A: Donna/hon o/agemashita ka.
B: Eigo no/hon o/agemashita.
A: Donna/kutsu o/agemashita ka.
B: Kireina/kutsu o/agemashita.

L16–1
1. (Issho ni) doraibu ni/ikima/sen ka.
2. Ee, zehi. (Ee, yorokonde. Ii desu ne. Ee, ikimashō.)
3. Doko ni/ikima/shō ka.
4. Hakone ni/ikima/sen ka. (Hakone wa/dō desu ka.)
5. Ee, sō shima/shō.

L16–2
Sample dialogue
1. Dō-yōbi ni (issho ni) ban-gohan o/tabemasen ka.
2. Ee, zehi. (Ee, yorokonde; Ii desu ne; Ee, tabemashō.)
3. Nani o/tabemashō ka.
4. Tempura o/tabemasen ka. (Tempura wa/dō desu ka.)
5. Ii desu/ne.
6. Nan-ji ni/aimashō ka.
7. Go-ji ni/aimasen ka. (Go-ji wa/dō desu ka.)
8. Ee, sō shima/shō.
9. Jā, do-yōbi/ni.
10. Jā, mata.

L16–3
Sample dialogue
1. Nichi-yōbi ni/ban-gohan o/tabemasen ka.

2. Zannen/desu ga, tsugō ga/warui desu.

3. Jā, do-yōbi ni/ikimasen ka.

4. Do-yōbi mo/tsugo ga warui desu.

5. Ja, kin-yōbi wa/dō desu ka.

6. Sumimasen, kin-yōbi mo chotto...

7. Sō desu/ka...

8. Jā, getsu-yōbi ni/ikimashō ka.

9. Ee, zehi!

L17

Sample dialogue

1. Dō/shimashita ka.

2. Kusuri o/agemashō ka.

3. Ee, onegai/shimasu.

4. Mizu o/agemashō ka.

5. Ee, onegaishimasu.

6. Eakon o/keshimashō ka.

7. Ee, onegaishimasu.

8. Mado o/akemashō ka.

9. Ee, onegaishimasu.

10. Dōmo-arigatō/gozaimasu.

11. Iie, dō itashi/mashite.

L18–1

1. Bijī-san wa/kuruma ga/arimasu.

2. (Bijī-san wa/)uchi ga/arimasu.

3. (Bijī-san wa/)o-kane ga/arimasu.

4. (Bijī-san wa/)yotto ga/arimasu.

5. (Bijī-san wa/)tomodachi ga/takusan/arimasu.

6. (Bijī-san wa/)eiga no/kippu ga/ni-mai/arimasu.

7. (Bijī-san wa/)imōto ga/hitori/arimasu.

8. (Bijī-san wa/)otōto ga/futari/arimasu.

L18-2

Hofuman-san wa/musuko-san ga/futari to/musume-san ga/hitori/arimasu. Ue no/musuko-san wa/nijū/go-sai desu. Shita no/musuko-san wa/hatachi desu. Musume-san wa/jūroku-sai/desu.

L18–3

1. Raishū/depāto de/bāgen/sērū ga/arimasu.

2. Ashita/Nihon Kaikan de/konsāto ga/arimasu.

3. Rainen/Ōsuto/raria de/gorufu/tōnamento ga/arimasu.

4. Sen/kyūhyaku/nanajū/ni-nen ni/Hokkaidō de/Orinpikku ga/arimashita.

5. Sen/kyūhyaku/hachijū/roku-nen ni/Tōkyō de/samitto ga/arimashita.

L18–4

Sample statements

1. Getsu-yōbi no/ku-ji kara/jūichi-ji made/kaisha de/kaigi ga/arimasu. Jūni-ji kara/Tōkyō/Hoteru de/Sumisu-san to/hiru-gohan o/tabemasu. Yo-ji kara /Rondon/Shōken no/Tōkyō/shisha de/kaigi ga/arimasu.

2. Ka-yōbi no/shichi-ji kara/Hakone no/gorufu/kurabu de/gorufu o/shimasu. Go-ji ni/kaisha ni/denwa o/shimasu.
   Soshite, hachi-ji kara/jū-ji made/gorufu/kurabu no/chikaku no/resu-

toran de/bangohan o/tabemasu.
3. Sui-yōbi no/ichi-ji kara/ni-ji made/Ōsaka/shisha de/kaigi ga/arimasu.
Yo-ji ni/Ōsaka/kōjō ni/ikimasu.
Shichi-ji kara/hachi-ji han made/Ōsaka/Hoteru de/bangōhan o/tabemasu.
Ku-ji kara/Ōsaka/Kurabu de/pātī ga/arimasu.
4. Moku-yōbi no/jū-ji kara/jūichi-ji han made/Kyōto/shisha de/kaigi ga/arimasu.
Jūni-ji kara/Kyōto no/resutoran de/hirugohan o/tabemasu.
Roku-ji kara/Yamada-san no/sōbetsu/kai ga/arimasu.
5. Kin-yōbi no/jūni-ji kara/hisho to/hirugohan o/tabemasu.
Yo-ji kara/ABC de/Hayashi-san ni/aimasu.
Roku-ji kara/Amerika/Taishikan de/pātī ga/arimasu.
6. Do-yōbi no/ichi-ji kara/Ginza de/kaimono o/shimasu.
Roku-ji kara/hachi-ji made/Ginza/Hōru de/konsāto ga/arimasu.
7. Nichi-yōbi no/ku-ji kara/jūichi-ji made/tomodachi to/kōen de/tenisu o/
shimasu.
Ni-ji kara/uchi de/pātī o/shimasu.
Shichi-ji kara/Tōkyō/Hoteru de/kekkon/shiki ga/arimasu.

L19–1

1. Bijī-san wa/kaisha ni/itte, kaigi o/shimasu.
Ginza ni/itte, tomodachi ni/aimasu.
Roppongi ni/itte, ban-gohan o/tabete, uchi ni/kaerimasu.
2. Bijī-san wa/kaisha ni/itte, kaigi o/shite, Ginza ni/ikimasu.
Tomodachi ni/atte, Roppongi ni/ikimasu.
Ban-gohan o/tabete, uchi ni/kaerimasu.
3. Bijī-san wa/kaisha ni/itte, /Roppongi ni/itte, uchi ni/kaerimasu.

L19–2

1. tabete	2. mite	3. tsukete	4. akete
5. agete	6. moratte	7. katte	8. atte
9. sutte	10. matte	11. kaette	12. itte
13. yonde	14. nonde	15. kaite	16. kiite
17. keshite	18. tenisu o/shite	19. kite	

L19–3

1. Kaigi no/mae ni/shokuji o/shimasu.
2. Kaigi no/ato de/repōto o/kakimasu.
3. Kaigi no/mae ni/kopī o/shimasu.
4. Kaigi no/ato de/repōto o/yomimasu.
5. Pātī no/mae ni/hana o/kaimasu.
6. Pātī no/ato de/uchi ni/kaerimasu.
7. Pātī no/mae ni/saka-ya ni/ikimasu.
8. Pātī no/ato de/denwa-bangō o/kikimasu.

L19–4

1. Kinō/tomodachi no/Rinda-san ga/Nihon ni/kimashita.
Rinda-san wa/konshū no/kin-yōbi made/Tōkyō ni/imasu.
Tōkyō ni/mikka dake/imasu. Shigoto desu/kara.

Sorekara, Sumisu-san to/issho ni/Nara ni/itte, furui/o-tera ya/niwa o/
mimasu. Nara ni/itsuka/imasu.
Sorekara, Ōsaka ni/itte/tomodachi ni/aimasu. Ōsaka ni/futsuka dake/imasu.
Soshite, Rinda-san wa/raishū no/do-yōbi ni/Amerika ni/kaerimasu.

L20–1

1. Menyū o/onegaishimasu (misete/kudasai)
2. Mizu o/onegaishimasu. (kudasai)
3. Naifu to/fōku o/onegaishimasu. (kudasai)
4. O-cha o/onegaishimasu. (kudasai)
5. O-kanjō o/onegaishimasu.

L20–2

1. Kēki o/onegai shimasu.
   Kōhī o/futatsu/onegaishimasu.
   Sando/itchi o/mittsu/onegaishimasu.
   Jūsu o/yottsu/onegaishimasu.
   Sarada o/futatsu/onegaishimasu.
   Bīru o/onegaishimasu.
2. Kēki to/kōhī o/futatsu/onegaishimasu.
3. Sandoitchi o/mittsu to/jūsu o/yottsu/onegaishimasu.
4. Kōhī o/futatsu to/sandoitchi o/mittsu to/sarada o/futatsu to/bīru o/hitotsu/
   one gaishimasu. Kōhī wa/ato de/onegaishimasu.

L20–3

Kuroi/beddo to/aoi/sofā to/shiroi/tana to/ōkii/terebi to/kuroi/denki-/sutando
o/todokete/kudasai. Sorekara, akai/kusshon o/futatsu/todokete/kudasai.
Raishū no/nichi-yōbi ni/onegaishimasu.

L20-4

Mikkusu piza o/futatsu to/sarada o/mittsu to/bīru o/mittsu/todokete/
kudasai.
Dekiru dake/hayaku/onegaishimasu.

L20–5

1. Bīru o/ichi-dāsu/jū-ji made ni/todokete/kudasai.
2. Ringo o/ichi-kiro/ni-ji made ni/uchi ni/todokete/kudasai.
3. Sarada/oiru o/go-hon/shichi-ji made ni/todokete/kudasai.
4. Mineraru-/uōtā o/roppon to/miruku o/san-bon/san-ji made ni/todokete/
   kudasai.
5. Hyaku-guramu/roppyaku-en no/gyūniku o/ni-kiro to/tamago o/ni-pakku/
   yo-ji made ni/todokete/kudasai.

L21-1

1. shingō   2. kado   3. kōsaten

L21-2

1. (1) Hidari ni/magatte/kudasai.

(2) Massugu/itte/kudasai.

(3) Migi ni/magatte/kudasai.

2. (1) Tsugi no/kado o/hidari ni/magatte/kudasai.

(2) Futatsu-me no/kado o/migi ni/magatte/kudasai.

3. (1) Ginkō no/saki de/tomete/kudasai.

(2) Ginkō no/mae de/tomete/kudasai.

(3) Ginkō no/temae de/tomete/kudasai.

4. (1) Tsugi no/kado o/migi ni/magatte/kudasai.

(2) Tsugi no/kado o/hidari ni/magatte/kudasai.

(3) Kōsaten o/massugu/itte/kudasai.

(4) Ginkō no/saki de/tomete/kudasai.

5. (1) Hidari ni/itte/kudasai.

(2) Migi ni/itte/kudasai.

L22–1

1. Basu ni/norimasu.	Basu o/orimasu.
2. Takushī ni/norimasu.	Takushī o/orimasu.
3. Densha ni/norimasu.	Densha o/orimasu.
4. Kaisha ni/tsukimasu.	Kaisha o/demasu.
5. Eki ni/tsukimasu.	Eki o/demasu.
6. Kūkō ni/tsukimasu.	Kūkō o/demasu.

L22–2

1. Shibuya de/densha ni/notte, Shinjuku de/orimasu.

2. Shibuya kara/Shinjuku made/juppun/kakarimasu.

3. Ginza de/basu ni/notte, Tōkyō de/orimasu.

4. Ginza kara/Tōkyō made/nijūgo-fun/kakarimasu.

5. Tōkyō de/Shinkansen ni/notte, Ōsaka de/orimasu.

6. Tōkyō kara/ Ōsaka made/san-jikan/kakarimasu.

L22–3

1. A: Ogikubo kara/Ginza made/dōyatte/ikimasu ka.

B: Ogikubo de/Marunouchi-sen ni/notte, Ginza de/orimasu.

A: Donogurai/kakarimasu ka.

B: Sanjuppun gurai/kakarimasu.

2. A: Ogikubo kara Ōtemachi made/dōyatte/ikimasu ka.

B: Ogikubo de/Tōzai-sen ni/notte, Ōtemachi de/orimasu.

A: Donogurai/kakarimasu ka.

B: Sanjuppun gurai/kakarimasu.

3. A: Ogikubo kara/Roppongi made/dōyatte/ikimasu ka.

B: Ogikubo de/Marunouchi-sen ni/notte, Kasumigaseki de/orimasu.

Kasumigaseki de/Hibiya-sen ni/norikaete, Roppongi de/orimasu.

A: Donogurai/kakarimasu ka.

B: Sanjūgo-fun gurai/kakarimasu.

4. A: Ogikubo kara/Asakusa made/dōyatte/ikimasu ka.

B: Ogikubo de/Marunouchi-sen ni/notte, Ginza de/orimasu.

Ginza de/Ginza-sen ni/norikaete, Asakusa de/orimasu.

A: Donogurai/kakarimasu ka.

B: Gojuppun gurai/kakarimasu.

L23–1
1. Terebi o/tsukete mo/ii desu ka.
2. Terebi o/keshite mo/ii desu ka.
3. Daidokoro ni/haitte mo/ii desu ka.
4. Shashin o/totte mo/ii desu ka.
5. Mado o/akete mo/ii desu ka.
6. Mado o/shimete mo/ii desu ka.

L23–2
1. A: Koko de (kono kaigi-shitsu de) /Nihon-go no/benkyō o/shite mo/ii desu ka.
   B: Ee, dōzo.
2. A: Koko de/ongaku o/kiite mo/ii desu ka.
   B: Sumimasen ga, sore wa/chotto...
3. A: Koko de/bīru o/nonde mo/ii desu ka.
   B: Sumimasen ga, sore wa/chotto...
4. A: Koko de/tabako o/sutte mo/ii desu ka.
   B: Ee, dōzo.
5. A: Koko de/terebi o/mite mo/ii desu ka.
   B: Sumimasen ga, sore wa/chotto...
6. A: Koko de/hiru-gohan o/tabete mo/ii desu ka.
   B: Sumimasen ga, sore wa/chotto...

L23–3
1. (1) Go-jūsho to o-namae o onegaishimasu.
   (2) Sumimasen. Pen ga arimasen.
   (3) Kono pen o tsukatte mo ii desu ka.
   (4) Hai, dōzo.
2. (1) Ashita ni-ji goro denwa o shite mo ii desu ka.
   (2) Sumimasen ga, [watashi wa] ni-ji goro uchi ni imasen kara, roku-ji goro onegaishimasu.
   (3) Hai, wakarimashita.

L23–4
1. Arubamu desu ka. Mite mo/ii desu ka.
2. Furansu no/wain desu ne. Nonde mo/iidesu ka.
3. Sutoroberī/kēki desu ne. Tabete mo/ii desu ka.
4. Watashi no/sukina/shīdī desu. Kiite mo/ii desu ka.
5. Kireina/kurisumasu/tsurī desu ne. Denki o/tsukete mo/ii desu ka.
6. Watashi ni/purezento desu ka. Akete mo/ii desu ka.

L24–1
1. Akenaide/kudasai.
2. Kesanaide/kudasai.
3. Konaide/kudasai.
4. Tomenaide/kudasai.
5. Ikanaide/kudasai.
6. Kawanaide/kudasai.
7. Toranaide/kudasai.

L24–2
1. Gomi-bako o/okanaide/kudasai.
2. Gomi o/sutenaide/kudasai.
3. Tatanaide/kudasai.   4. Osanaide/kudasai.
5. Fumanaide/kudasai.   6. Warawanaide/kudasai.
7. Okoranaide/kudasai.   8. Nakanaide/kudasai.

L24–3
1. A: Terebi o/tsukete mo/ii desu ka.
   B: Sumimasen ga, tsukenaide/kudasai. Urusai/desu kara.
2. A: Terebi o/keshite mo/ii desu ka.
   B: Sumimasen ga, kesanaide/kudasai. Omoshiroi/desu kara.
3. A: Daidokoro ni/haitte mo/ii desu ka.
   B: Sumimasen ga, hairanaide/kudasai.   Kireidewa/arimasen/kara.
4. A: Shashin o/totte mo/ii desu ka.
   B: Sumimasen ga, toranaide/kudasai. Kireidewa/arimasen/kara.
5. A: Mado o/akete mo/ii desu ka.
   B: Sumimasen ga, akenaide/kudasai. Urusai/desu kara.
6. A: Mado o/shimete mo/ii desu ka.
   B: Sumimasen ga, shimenaide/kudasai. Atsui/desu kara.

L25–1
1. (1) Tabemasu.   (2) Tabete imasu.   (3) Tabemashita.
2. (1) Sōji o/shimasu.   (2) Sōji o/shite imasu.   (3) Sōji o/shimashita.
3. (1) Nomimasu.   (2) Nonde imasu.   (3) Nomimashita.
4. (1) Kirimasu.   (2) Kitte imasu.   (3) Kirimashita.

L25–2
1. Katō-san wa/denwa o/shite imasu.
2. Suzuki-san wa/kiite imasu.
3. Nakamura-san wa/shimbun o/yonde imasu.
4. Itō-san wa/matte imasu.
5. Yoshiko-san wa/kopī o/shite imasu.
6. Watanabe-san wa/tabako o/sutte imasu.
7. Tanaka-san wa/aruite/imasu.
8. Kondō-san wa/kaigi o/shite imasu.
9. Hayashi-san wa/setsumei o/shite imasu.
10. Yoshida-san wa/kōhī o/nonde imasu.
11. Harada-san wa/kēki o/tabete imasu.
12. Satō-san wa/nete imasu.
13. Sasaki-san wa/shashin o/mite imasu.
14. Andāson-san wa/shashin o/misete imasu.
15. Mariko-san wa/Ei-go de/hanashi o/shite imasu.
16. Yamada-san wa/tegami o/kaite imasu.

L26
1. Moshi moshi, Suzuki desu ga, Buraun-san no o-taku desu ka.

2. A, Suzuki-san, konbanwa.
3. Buraun-san, raishū no do-yōbi no ban, watashi no uchi de pātī o shimasu.
   Watashi no tanjōbi no pātī desu.
4. Okusan to issho ni kimasen ka.
5. Dōmo arigatō gozaimasu. Yorokonde ikimasu.
6. Dewa, do-yōbi ni.
   O-denwa dōmo arigatō gozaimashita.
7. Yoku irasshaimashita. Dōzo kochira ni.
8. Omaneki arigatō gozaimasu. Kore o dōzo.
9. Kireina hana desu ne. Dōmo arigatō gozaimasu.
10. Kono wain mo dōzo.
11. Mina-san ni go-shōkai shimasu kara, dōzo kochira ni.
12. Buraun-san, kuruma de kimashita ka.
    Iie, densha de kimashita.
13. Osoi desu kara, watashi no kuruma de kaerimasen ka.
    Sō desu ka. Arigatō gozaimasu. Onegaishimasu.
14. Totemo tanoshikatta desu. Kyō wa dōmo arigatō gozaimashita.
    Dō itashimashite. Watashi mo tanoshikatta desu. Mata kite kudasai.
15. Dōzo ki o tsukete.
16. Oyasumi nasai.
    Oyasumi nasai.

L27–1
  1. (1) Kekkon/shimasu.   (2) Kekkon/shimashita.   (3) Kekkon/shite imasu.
  2. (1) Nekutai o/shimasu. (2) Nekutai o/shimashita. (3) Nekutai o/shite imasu.
  3. (1) Kimasu.   (2) Kimashita.   (3) Kite imasu.

L27–2
  1. Hofuman-san wa/Berurin Ginkō ni/tsutomete imasu.
     Tōkyō ni/sunde imasu.
     Kekkon/shite imasu.
  2. Ue no/musuko-san mo/Berurin Ginkō ni/tsutomete imasu.
     Nyūyōku ni/sunde imasu.Kekkon/shite imasen.
  3. Shita no/musuko-san wa/ryokō-gaisha ni/tsutomete imasu.
     Honkon ni/sunde imasu.
     Kekkon/shite imasu.
  4. Ojō-san(musume-san) wa/gakusei desu.
     Berurin ni/sunde imasu.
     Kekkon/shite imasen.

L27–3
  1. Yoshida-san wa/konshū no/getsu-yōbi kara/raishū no/moku-yōbi made/
     Nyūyōku ni/itte imasu.
  2. Hayashi-san wa/konshū no/getsu-yōbi kara/raishū no/ka-yōbi made/
     Honkon ni/itte imasu.
  3. Katō-san wa/konshū no/ka-yōbi kara/raishū no/ka-yōbi made/Kyōto
     ni/itte imasu.
  4. Satō-san wa/kinō kara/raishū no/getsu-yōbi made/Nagoya ni/itte imasu.

178

5. Bijī-san wa/konshū no/sui-yōbi kara/raishū no/kin-yōbi made/Ōsaka ni/itte imasu.

6. Mariko-san wa/kinō kara/raishū no/kin-yōbi made Berurin ni/itte imasu.

L27–4

1. Satō-san wa/Shinjuku ni/sunde imasu.
   Tōkyō Denki ni/tsutomete imasu.
   Tanoshii/hito desu.

2. Bijī-san wa/Aoyama ni/sunde imasu.
   Nyūyōku Shōken ni/tsutomete imasu.
   Isogashii/hito desu.

3. Mariko-san wa/Ginza ni/sunde imasu.
   Nyūyōku Shōken ni/tsutomete imasu.
   Shinsetsuna/hito desu.

4. Fukuda-san wa/Azabu ni/sunde imasu.
   Berurin Ginkō ni/tsutomete imasu.
   Akarui/hito desu.

5. Kanda-san wa/Yokohama ni/sunde imasu.
   Tōkyō Denki ni/tsutomete imasu.
   Majimena/hito desu.

6. Junko-san wa/Asakusa ni/sunde imasu.
   Tōkyō Denki ni/tsutomete imasu.
   Nigiyakana/hito desu.

L28–1

1. (1) Satō-san wa/o-sake ga/suki desu.
   (2) Bijī-san wa/bīru ga/suki desu.
   (3) Junko-san wa/kōhī ga/suki desu.
   (4) Mariko-san wa/wain ga/suki desu.
2. (1) Satō-san wa/gorufu ga/jōzu desu.
   (2) Bijī-san wa/tenisu ga/jōzu desu.
   (3) Junko-san wa/sukī ga/jōzu desu.
   (4) Mariko-san wa/uta ga/jōzu desu.
3. (1) Satō-san wa/Ei-go ga/dekimasu.
   (2) Bijī-san wa/Nihon-go ga/dekimasu.
   (3) Junko-san wa/Furansu-go ga/dekimasu.
   (4) Mariko-san wa/Chūgoku-go ga/dekimasu.

L28–2

1. Terebi o/mitai desu.
3. Hon o/yomitai desu.
5. Kōhī o/nomitai desu.

2. Ongaku o/kikitai desu.
4. Sutēki o/tabetai desu.
6. Tenisu o/shitai desu.

L28-3

1. Dō shimashita ka.
3. Netsu ga arimasu ka.
5. Atama mo itai desu.
7. Hai, itai desu.

2. Kinō kara kibun ga warui desu.
4. Ee, sanjūkyū-do arimasu.
6. Nodo mo itai desu ka.

8. Kusuri o agemasu kara shokuji no ato de nonde kudasai. Dōzo o-daiji ni.

L29

Sample answer

Sumimasen, menyū o misete kudasai.

Hai, dōzo.

Nomimono wa nani ga ii desu ka.

Bīru ga ii desu.

Ryōri wa sukiyaki ga ii desu ka, shabushabu ga ii desu ka.

Sukiyaki wa senshū tabemashita kara, shabushabu ga ii desu.

Shokuji no ato de kōhī wa ikaga desu ka.

Hai, itadakimasu.

Bīru o ni-hon to shabushabu o onegaishimasu. Dezāto wa meron ga ii desu.

Hai, wakarimashita.

L30

Sample answer

1. Sumimasen, hanashi o/shite mo/ii desu ka.
   Watashi wa/Kyōto ni/ikimasu. Kyōto de/furui o-tera ya/kireina niwa o/mimasu.
2. O-tera wa/doko ga/ii desu ka. Hoteru wa/doko ga/ii desu ka. Resutoran wa/doko ga/ii desu ka.
3. Watashi wa/Bijī desu. Nyūyōku Shōken ni/tsutomete imasu. Shigoto wa/isogashii desu. Tōkyō ni/sunde imasu.
4. Mainichi/hachi-ji kara/shichi-ji goro made/shigoto o/shite imasu. Shūmatsu wa/tomodachi to/tenisu o/yoku shimasu. Watashi wa/tenisu ga/suki desu.
5. Shokudō-sha ni/ikimasen ka.
6. Kyō wa/domo/arigatō/gozaimashita. Totemo/tanoshikatta/desu.

The Authors: Registered with Japan's Ministry of Education as a nonprofit organization in 1977, AJALT was established to meet the needs of people who are not necessarily specialists on Japan but who wish to communicate effectively in Japanese. Along with private and group instruction at all levels, AJALT carries on research, develops teaching materials, and trains teachers of Japanese. Its instructors are often called on to provide their services and expertise to government agencies, foundations, and educational institutions. It was awarded the Japan Foundation Special Prize in 1992.

JAPANESE FOR BUSY PEOPLE I & II

Association for Japanese-Language Teaching (AJALT)

This two-volume language-learning program makes it possible to communicate naturally and effectively in both business and social contexts.

I TEXT: ISBN 0-87011-599-5; paperback; 216 pages
TAPES: ISBN 0-87011-637-1; four 30-minute tapes
COMPACT DISCS: ISBN 4-7700-1607-7; two discs
TEACHERS MANUAL: ISBN 4-7700-1608-5; paperback; 160 pages

II TEXT: ISBN 0-87011-919-2; paperback; 424 pages
TAPES: ISBN 0-87011-925-7; six 60-minute tapes

"POWER JAPANESE" SERIES

INSTANT VOCABULARY
Through Prefixes and Suffixes

Timothy J. Vance

Create new words from words you already know.
ISBN 0-87011-953-2; paperback; 128 pages

"BODY" LANGUAGE

Jeffrey G. Garrison

Master common idioms that refer to the body.
ISBN 0-87011-955-9; paperback; 128 pages

ALL ABOUT PARTICLES

Naoko Chino

Learn to use particles properly.
ISBN 0-87011-954-0; paperback; 128 pages

GONE FISHIN'
New angles on Perennial Problems

Jay Rubin

Clear up problematic aspects of learning Japanese.
ISBN 4-7700-1656-5; paperback; 128 pages

BEYOND POLITE JAPANESE

Akihiko Yonekawa

Get past textbook Japanese and speak like the natives do.
ISBN 4-7700-1539-9; paperback; 128 pages

ALL ABOUT KATAKANA

Anne Matsumoto Stewart

Conquer *katakana* quickly and efficiently.
ISBN 4-7700-1696-4; paperback; 128 pages